DIGITAL
PHOTOGRAPHY
STEP BY STEP

DIGITAL PHOTOGRAPHY
STEP BY STEP

BEN OWEN

ARCTURUS

ARCTURUS

Arcturus Publishing Limited
26/27 Bickels Yard
151–153 Bermondsey Street
London SE1 3HA

Published in association with
foulsham
W. Foulsham & Co. Ltd,
The Publishing House, Bennetts Close, Cippenham,
Slough, Berkshire SL1 5AP, England

ISBN- 13: 978-0-572-03196-1
ISBN- 10: 0-572-03196-3

This edition printed in 2006

British Library Cataloguing-in-Publication Data: a catalogue record for this
book is available from the British Library

Editor: Belinda Jones
Design: Talking Design

Printed in China

CONTENTS

Introduction 6

A Short History Lesson 8

Chapter One – A Digital Revolution 10
A Typical Digital Camera 12
The Advantages Of Digital Photography 14
The Disadvantages Of Digital Photography 14
How Is A Digital Camera Different? 14
How Does A Digital Camera Work? 15
Memory Cards 15
Pixels And Camera Quality 15
Megapixel Cameras 15

Chapter Two – The Digital Camera 16
What Digital Camera? 18
Choosing The Right Camera For Your Needs 18
Other Factors To Consider 19
Understanding Your Digital Camera 20
Typical Mode Dial Symbols 23
The Memory Card 22
Memory Card Options 23

Chapter Three – Taking Pictures 24
Some Basic Photographic Principles 26
Adding Impact To Your Shots 31
Composition 34
Portraits 37
Lighting 40
Flash Photography 41
Landscapes And Cityscapes 42
Panoramas 42
Colour 43
Using Colour 43
Movement 44

Chapter Four – From Camera To Computer 46
Choice Of Computer 48
Downloading To Your Computer 48

Chapter Five – The Editing Process 50
Calibrating Your Monitor 52
Your Software Choices 53
File Types 53
The Toolbar And Photoshop Elements Screen . . . 54
Opening An Image 55
Straightening And Cropping 57
Saving A File 58
Changing The Shape of Your Image 61
Image Stitching For Panoramas 62
Improving Your Images 64
Adjusting the Hue And Saturation 66
Selecting An Area Inside Your Image 67
Feathering 68
Colour Balance 70
Overexposure And Underexposure 72
The History Window 75
Layers 75
Unsharp Mask 78
Gaussian Blur 79
Text Tool 80
Colour To Black And White 81
Duotones 84
Cloning And Spot Healing 86
Red-Eye Reduction 87

Chapter Six – Printing Your Images 88
Printing Equipment And Facilities 90
Colour 90
Printing 91

Troubleshooting 92

A–Z Glossary 93

Index 95

INTRODUCTION

Welcome to this book and all the exciting possibilities digital photography has to offer.

Whether you have already bought, or have recently been given a digital camera; or if you are just thinking about making the leap, this book will provide you with all you need to know about to create great pictures.

Unlike some authors of similar publications, I do not intend to bamboozle you with complicated jargon. New technology in any form can be confusing so, without trying to patronize you, I will explain things as plainly as possible, using lots of example images. You will be provided with all the information you need to make you feel confident about using your digital camera and manipulating your images.

This book has been designed to accompany you every step of the way – from unwrapping your new camera to holding a tangible image in your hand, or sharing it online or even on your mobile phone.

In the first chapter the basic facts of digital photography will be explained to you. If you then turn to the second chapter, you will be given an overview of the digital camera itself. There are many digital cameras on the market, from the most basic to expensive, feature-rich models. However, they all operate in a similar way so much of the information in this section will relate directly to your own camera, what ever make or style it is. Understanding your camera and all of its features will allow you to make the most of it when you come to taking pictures.

The third chapter, called 'Taking Pictures', will perhaps be the most important part of this book in the eyes of many readers. In it, I will draw upon considered expert opinion as well as my own experience as I provide you with hints and advice that will enable you to create great pictures. All aspects of digital photography will be covered, from the basics to the ways in which you can get the most from any situation.

After you have taken your pictures you will need to know how to download them to your computer. Chapter Four deals with this part and also shows you how to organize your images. You can then move on to Chapter Five, which covers the digital 'darkroom'. Digital photography gives anyone with access to a computer the opportunity to develop and edit their own pictures without all the stains, smell and mess of a traditional darkroom. From simple procedures like cropping an image to more complicated, but easily mastered, actions such as converting your image into black and white, you will be guided closely through each stage.

Last but not least, the final chapter tells you how to print your photographs, and advises you on the best equipment for this stage to ensure perfect results.

The software that will be referred to in the book is Photoshop Elements as it is the software closest to being the industry standard.

My aim is that by the end of *Digital Photography Step by Step* you will feel that you are well on your way to being completely comfortable with your digital camera, and confident that you can achieve pleasing, professional-looking results with it every time.

A SHORT HISTORY LESSON

Starting with the earliest cave paintings, man has always tried to capture what he sees before him. This desire to express ourselves, to reproduce our own vision of the world, is deeply ingrained within us.

When photography was invented in the early part of the nineteenth century, people marvelled at the almost instantaneous reproduction of the world around them. No longer did they need the talent and the patience to painstakingly draw or paint what they saw. Painters like Cézanne and Monet scorned the invention. They were unable to understand why anyone would want a literal reproduction of their surroundings.

However, early master photographers like Jacques-Henri Lartigue celebrated the ability of photography to capture movement and the 'instant'. Fascinated by photography from the age of five, Lartigue had long realized what a camera could do.

The invention of the box Brownie, patented by Kodak at the turn of the twentieth century, allowed ordinary people to take pictures. Before then, photography had been the province of the wealthy. Photography exploded in popularity giving, as it did, everyone the opportunity to become an artist.

Photographs can now be counted among our most prized possessions. How many people say that the family albums would be the first treasures that they would attempt to save in the event of a fire?

Despite its popularity, however, film-based photography has two main disadvantages. The first drawback is the cost – to buy a 36-exposure roll of film and afterwards get it printed and developed can be expensive; enough to limit the images you might have taken had it all been free. And you cannot be sure that the pictures on the film are even worth developing.

The second disadvantage is the possibility of getting home to discover that the potentially wonderful holiday pictures of your nearest and dearest are bleached out or out of focus. Even worse, the lens cap might have been on all the time, leaving you staring at blank images.

The advent of digital photography has consigned all of these problems to the past.

A DIGITAL REVOLUTION

The amateur photographer is now able to choose from an extensive and increasingly affordable range of digital cameras. In fact, it is probably true to say that a photographic revolution has taken place. The impact of this digital revolution has perhaps been as great as that of the introduction of the Kodak box Brownie, just under a century ago.

Although the initial cost of a digital camera is somewhat higher than that of a traditional 35mm film camera (the gap is rapidly closing, however), you can then record millions of images without paying a single penny more – if you don't want to print your photographs, that is.

1.0 A DIGITAL REVOLUTION

A TYPICAL DIGITAL CAMERA

Some features you might expect to find on your digital camera.

Back of camera

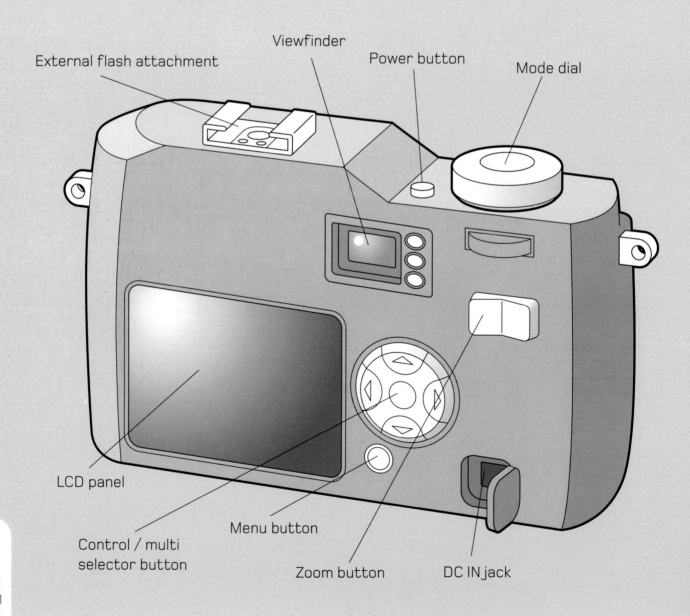

External flash attachment

Viewfinder

Power button

Mode dial

LCD panel

Menu button

Control / multi
selector button

Zoom button

DC IN jack

Front of camera

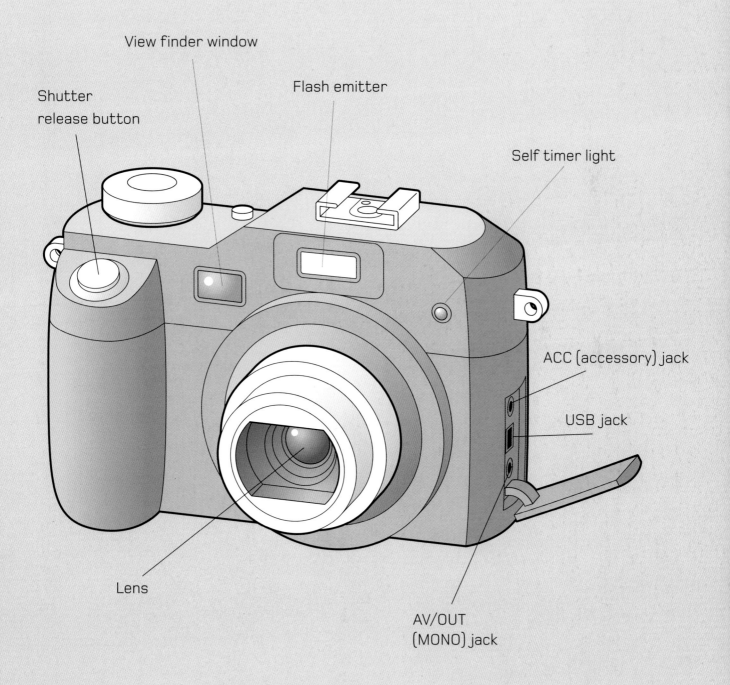

View finder window

Flash emitter

Shutter
release button

Self timer light

ACC (accessory) jack

USB jack

Lens

AV/OUT
(MONO) jack

THE ADVANTAGES OF DIGITAL PHOTOGRAPHY

- you can take as many photographs in one go as your memory card will allow (see page 22)
- you can review what you have taken immediately
- both of the above factors give you the ability to experiment with what you take
- digital cameras offer much more versatility and convenience, allowing you to do so much more
- print quality is usually just as good as digital's 35mm rivals, as long as you don't intend to print larger than A3 size
- there is no need for your own computer (though it does help) because there are many places that can print your images; even convenient, hole-in-the-wall places are emerging
- you can send your images around the world at the touch of a button via email and even your mobile phone
- there is the added convenience of not having to carry roll after roll of film around with you on holiday
- in the long run, digital photography is relatively cheaper though this, of course, depends on how many images you want to print.

THE DISADVANTAGES OF DIGITAL PHOTOGRAPHY

- camera battery life is limited due to the abundance of computerized parts
- there can be difficulty in picking up a sharp difference between light and dark
- the LCD (liquid crystal display) viewfinder can sometimes be hard to see on a bright day
- the 'shutter lag' – the delay between pressing the shutter button and actually capturing the image can lead to missed opportunities (see page 20)
- the initial cost of a digital camera and one or two memory cards is higher than traditional 35mm camera and film.

The limitations of using a digital camera will be addressed throughout the book, and you will be offered hints and suggestions on how to negate them.

Perhaps the greatest problem with digital photography is getting to grips with the new technology. It can seem like an insurmountable task when you are faced with all the buttons, menus, options, software and such like – but you have a headstart because this book will take you through it all and show you how easy it really is.

HOW IS A DIGITAL CAMERA DIFFERENT?

The film-based photographic process begins when light enters a lens and strikes light-sensitive film (the negative), changing the composition of the emulsion on the film. The action of the film developing chemicals then triggers off coloured dyes in the emulsion which procduces the negative image.

A digital camera replaces traditional film with an electronic sensor that is made up of millions of tiny light-sensitive dots which then stores the image using the same binary code (1s and 0s) as a computer. This information is stored on the memory card inside your camera, which you (or your local developers) can then copy to a computer – this is called downloading.

Traditional camera	Digital camera
FILM	MEMORY CARD
IMAGE IS TAKEN	IMAGE IS TAKEN
TAKEN TO A PROCESSOR	DOWNLOADED ONTO A COMPUTER
DEVELOPED AND PRINTED	EDITED AND PRINTED

HOW DOES A DIGITAL CAMERA WORK?

Light enters the camera through the lens and hits the camera's sensor. The sensor is made up of millions of pixels, and each pixel is made up of a coloured filter of reds, greens and blues. By a process called 'colour interpolation', the light that hits these pixels is turned into the image's colours. These building blocks of original colour are then converted into digital data by the computer chips inside the camera, and the final image is then constructed, to be sent to the memory card where it is stored.

Digital cameras are examined in more detail in Chapter Two, page 18.

MEMORY CARDS

A memory card is an electronic chip inside a plastic cover which stores data and image information – it is often referred to as 'digital film'. There are many different types so although a card with a small memory capacity should come with the camera, be careful you get the right one when buying further cards.

See page 22 for more details on memory cards.

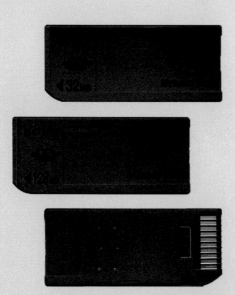

PIXELS AND CAMERA QUALITY

The word 'pixel' is short for pixel element – the building blocks of your image.

One of the problems with digital photography is understanding the differences in quality you get from different cameras. Image quality used to depend on a camera's lens and other features. While these are still important aspects to consider, with digital photography the first thing to understand is the role pixels play in determining the quality of your final picture.

Generally the more pixels the image has, the better the quality and sharpness of the image. Do remember this, because this point has an impact on any editing decisions you may be called upon to make later on. So, when deciding on which camera to buy you will need to see the difference an increasing number of pixels can give you.

MEGAPIXEL CAMERAS

All digital cameras are what is called 'megapixel' cameras.

Nowadays, even most phone cameras have a capacity of one megapixel, and you should be looking for a camera with a much higher pixel capacity. Even two megapixels is at the bottom end of the market these days – these simple cameras will produce adequate prints up to postcard size, and images suitable for emailing, web sites and the internet.

You should be looking at a camera with a capacity of more than three or four megapixels. Images from these cameras are capable of being printed to a size of over 8 x 10 inches (203 x 255mm) while retaining photographic quality.

There are also other factors to consider when thinking about the quality of your images, such as the lens and the camera's processor. These will be discussed on page 19 and 20, but it is important that you understand the idea behind these pixels and how they affect the quality of the image.

THE DIGITAL CAMERA

Though a not entirely different beast from anything you will have used in the past – you still press a shutter button to take a picture – it is important to acquaint yourself with the differences that the digital revolution has brought to cameras.

With dozens of brands competing for your custom you will need to know how they differ from each other. After you have made your purchase you will then need to be aware of what your camera is capable of doing.

2.0 THE DIGITAL CAMERA

WHAT DIGITAL CAMERA?

The first thing you need to decide is what you are using your camera for.

Points to consider:

- what will you do with your images? Will your prints be large or small?
- do you need an expensive, high-quality camera? If you only need to use it for small email attachments or postcard-sized prints or images then you don't need thousands of pounds worth of equipment
- do you want to just point and shoot or would you like the chance to explore and experiment once you are more comfortable with the process? Some, but not all, cameras offer a totally manual option that makes experimental photography possible
- weight and size of camera
- type and brand of lens
- the feel of the camera – is it comfortable?

> **Remember: You can only reduce the size of your image to fit any size (postcard or giant poster) or fit any medium (mobile phone, email, newsletter, glossy brochure or family print) – you can't enlarge it. Therefore, the more megapixels you have the better the quality of the image and the more flexible your options are.**

CHOOSING THE RIGHT CAMERA FOR YOUR NEEDS

There are three basic types of digital camera.

The first and most common type is the compact camera – these are popular with the mass-market and are often the smallest and simplest.

The second alternative is what is known as a prosumer or bridge camera. These will often offer better lenses, allowing a greater focal length and excellent macro abilities for wildlife photographs. They are simpler and increasingly cheaper than their SLR (Single Lens Reflex) rivals.

Finally there is the SLR, which is the most expensive choice. With this one, you have all the features you need and also interchangeable lenses. You need to decide which type fulfils your needs the best.

Most digital cameras these days offer at least three megapixels. You can, as you have seen, pick up cheaper models for between £50 and £100 which offer perfectly acceptable images but these are only really suitable for small email attachments and your mobile phone.

3–4 MP	Great for beginners. These are found at the lower end of the market, which means fewer options/features. Ideal for perfect prints of 6 x 4 inches (153 x 103mm). Prices range from £100–£300 depending on size, weight, features and the brand.
5 MP	Slightly more detail offering you greater quality and therefore the chance to print excellent images up to 8 x 6 inches (204 x 153mm).
7+MP	Prices can be as low as £150 and can rise to £450. Great detail and ideal for printing A4 and upwards; perfect for framing on your wall. Prices start at £300 and rise to the high levels of the professional market.

OTHER FACTORS TO CONSIDER

LENSES

Perhaps as important as the pixels issue is how well the camera 'sees' the image. Most compact cameras offer zoom lenses, but some picture quality can be seen to have been sacrificed when compared to the optics inside the fixed or prime lens of an SLR. How the lens is made is also very important, as is how it deals with problems such as flare and image distortion. And always consider what aperture size it gives you (see page 27). I would instinctively choose lenses from traditional camera makers rather than those newer to the market.

OPTICAL vs DIGITAL ZOOM

The focal length influences the range and perspective of the lens. Most digital cameras have an optical zoom lens which offers the option of a short focal length for landscapes and moves through to a long focal length that can photograph detail on a building, for example.

When a digital camera incorporates a 'digital zoom' it means that once the optical zoom has reached its largest focal length, the digital zoom will then crop in and enlarge the middle part of the frame. This is the same as cropping the middle section of an image on your computer, but be aware that this reduces the quality and consequently the size of the image. The only real advantage is that this enables you to see the crop on your LCD viewfinder rather than having to wait until you or the developers enlarge it.

Be careful when a camera offers you, for example, an optical zoom of 3x and a digital zoom of 5x. This does not mean that the camera's maximum focal length is eight times its smallest (i.e. 35mm to 280mm). What it simply means is that its largest focal length is three times its smallest. This is what many compact cameras have; they offer the 35mm equivalent of 35 to 105mm.

Look at these two shots (left and right) of a hunt in Hertfordshire, England, to see how different focal lengths affect a picture. The left is shot with a 16mm lens whilst the right is shot with a 200mm lens

An optical zoom is the actual zoom; a digital zoom is simply a 'crop' into the image, reducing the size and quality of the file. This image (left) is a digital zoom of the image above left. It is probably at the largest size of reproduction possible; any larger, and the image would suffer in terms of quality

THE PROCESSOR

The processor determines what the camera does with the pixels it has. It turns the raw data that it receives into a proper photograph. All of the aspects that make up a powerful image such as the contrast, detail, sharpness and tonal range are all dependent on the processor.

EXPOSURE MODES

All compact cameras will offer you auto-exposure modes. (Exposure is the balance between the correct aperture and the shutter speed – see page 29.) But not all cameras offer you the chance to manually adjust these settings. This is important because the camera can often get it wrong and you will often want to take control of your pictures.

TYPE OF VIEWFINDER

The principal way of looking at your proposed subject and composing an image can be different from that of a traditional camera. Instead of looking through an eyepiece, you are encouraged to look through a LCD screen. Some digital cameras don't even have an eyepiece, so check on this if that is your preferred way of composing. Also, some cameras have hinged LCD viewfinders which are very useful for composing over people's heads in a crowd, or for self-portraits.

UNDERSTANDING YOUR DIGITAL CAMERA

A complete understanding of all the knobs, buttons and features on your camera is vital before you start.

Though there are many different makes and models of camera on the market today, they all share common features you can look at now.

POWER ON/OFF

This can take a moment or two to come on so don't force it. Most models will turn off automatically if left on for too long.

SHUTTER BUTTON

This takes the picture. Usually this is a two stage process: press halfway down to focus the subject (when you should hear a little beep saying your subject is in focus) and then press all the way down to capture the image.

> Remember: On most of the mass-market compact cameras there is a short time-delay between pressing the shutter button and the image being captured – the 'shutter lag'. You will have to learn the length of this delay in order to take effective sports or action pictures otherwise the subject will be long gone by the time you have captured the image.

LCD SCREEN

This is the main hub of operations and navigating it may at first seem difficult, but it will become second nature once you get the hang of it. Its principal purpose is to act as a viewfinder (displaying exactly what you want to capture). Though this is different from the traditional way of composing and may take time to get used to, it does offer the advantage of viewing the image you are about to take more fully. Most cameras will offer you the traditional eyepiece, though not all.

The LCD screen also displays a menu of the camera's features. These are usually divided into three sections.

- PLAYBACK mode. Allows you to review your images and either delete them or move them into various folders.

- RECORD mode. Determines how the picture is taken in terms of the white balance, the metering, the ISO, the image quality, etc.

- SET-UP options. Used for language settings, the date and time, etc.

Many of these options will have default settings which are the standard modes that are set up by the camera manufacturer.

Remember: Try to use the LCD screen as little as possible because it can reduce battery life very quickly.

One of the clever things about digital cameras is that you can change the settings in between shots, rather than having to change the whole film. This is especially useful in terms of the white balance and ISO settings.

WHITE BALANCE
Different light sources produce different colours – a lamp will produce warmer light while daylight produces colder colours. You need to set the camera according to what you are photographing – all cameras will have an auto-white balance setting but many offer a manual mode with a range from sunny to cloudy to artificial light.

ISO
The ISO setting determines how sensitive the sensor is to light. At 100 ISO the sensor is less sensitive to light, so this setting is best used on bright days: a setting of 400 ISO is much more light sensitive and is best used for indoor photography. Most compact cameras will offer you a range of 100–400 ISO, though more advanced cameras will go up to 1600.

METERING
Many cameras offer a choice of spot metering and evaluative metering.

Spot metering bases the correct exposure on a given area or 'spot' in the frame.

Evaluative metering uses the entire frame to set the correct exposure – a compromise that includes all the varying degrees of light.

CONTROL DIAL
This comes in many shapes and sizes. It allows you to navigate your way through the menu options.

FLASH
Most cameras have a built-in flash. Flash and the successful use of it will be discussed on page 41.

PORTS
These are connections to various outlets – a slot for your memory card; a USB (universal serial bus) for downloads to your computer; a DC port for recharging from the mains socket and an AV/ OUT connection to your television.

MODE DIAL
Again these come in different shapes and are often found around the shutter button. All will move you through the different camera modes – from auto through to the manual settings (see overleaf and page 30 for further details on the settings).

Volcano, sunset, Equador. ISO 1600

Remember: As the ISO increases so the quality of the image decreases. Greater sensitivity to light means greater 'noise' or 'grain' in your image.

TYPICAL MODE DIAL SYMBOLS

M
Manual

A
Aperture
priority

S
Shutter
priority

P
Program

Auto

SCN

Portrait

Landscape

Action

Macro

Short film
capacity

Display
images

THE MEMORY CARD: 'THE ENDLESSLY RE-USABLE ROLL OF FILM'

Unlike a traditional camera where film is used, developed and then thrown away (or kept if copies or enlargements are wanted), the 'digital film' or memory card can be re-used as many times as you wish.

The memory card, which comes in different shapes and sizes, is essentially an electronic chip inside a plastic cover. As you have seen in How Does A Digital Camera Work? (page 15) the memory card stores the image information or data that has been captured and interpreted by the camera.

Each memory card has a set amount of space which will capture a given number of images depending on the quality setting in your camera. The higher the quality – or number of megapixels used – the fewer the images that can be recorded. Once the card is full you can then copy your images to a computer or take them to a developing outlet. The card should then be erased and can then be used again.

The erasing of the information on the card is called formatting – the formatting button on your camera is usually found within the menu options. When you get a new card you should format it immediately and then each time you copy the information to your computer.

DOWNLOADING

This is the term used to describe the process of copying the information you have on your memory card, in this case photographs, to a computer. Uploading is the opposite of this – from the computer to a memory card. This is useful if you have a computer but not a printer – you can edit your images and then upload or copy them to a memory card before handing them to a developer to complete the job.

BE CAREFUL! DON'T FORMAT THE CARD UNTIL YOU HAVE DOWNLOADED THE IMAGES ON IT

If you delete an image by accident or format your memory card while it is full, there is software available to rescue the images: there may even be an undo command on your camera. While the card may appear to be totally erased, the file data often remains intact because only the filing system is erased. This means images can be rescued.

Possible software options: FUJIFILM IMAGE
RECOVERY
BOOMERANG
PHOTORESCUE
SANDISK RESCUEPRO
IMAGERECALL

A quick search on an internet search engine will give you any number of other options.

MEMORY CARD OPTIONS

There are many different types of memory card and although they shouldn't really influence your choice of camera, it is wise to know the differences. Also, while a small capacity memory card should come with the camera, be careful you get the right one when buying further ones.

COMPACT FLASH: these are the most common. They are relatively inexpensive, and offer large spaces: up to 4GB (4000MB).

MICRODRIVE: these fragile objects contain small hard-drives. In my experience they are too delicate to be useful even if they offer more for less than Compact Flash cards.

SMART MEDIA: these are lightweight but fragile.

MEMORY STICK: these are mainly used in some products more than others. I find they can be on the small side.

SECURE DIGITAL: like the Memory Stick they are widely used but more expensive than Compact Flash cards.

xD PICTURE CARD: these are the smallest cards and they offer the largest capacity for memory.

> **Remember: All memory cards are relatively expensive – you don't want to keep replacing them as they are designed to be used over and over again. Therefore keep them away from magnetic fields, keep them free from dust by blowing on their contacts from time to time and keep them in their casing when not being used.**

TAKING PICTURES

Once you have got to grips with the technical stuff you can concentrate on the important and fun part – taking great pictures.

Before you look at some individual scenarios and how you might approach them, it is important to make sure that you understand some of the basic photographic principles. While you may just want to stick the camera on auto and let it do the work for you, I promise that the more you know, the more pleasure you will get out of making the camera work for you.

3.0 TAKING PICTURES

SOME BASIC PHOTOGRAPHIC PRINCIPLES

Correct exposure is the result of the right balance between the shutter speed and the aperture.

An image's depth of field is the area of sharpness in front of and behind the main focused area.

The flash is the camera's built-in source of artificial light.

The degree of image quality is determined by the lens, the ISO, adequate light, the number of megapixels and the size it is to be seen at – either on paper or on the screen.

SHUTTER SPEED

This is the speed at which the shutter opens and closes when it lets in the light needed to capture the image. The shutter speed you need depends on the light available and the subject you are photographing. If you are taking a landscape picture you don't need to use a very fast shutter speed, but if you are taking a picture of, for example, a football game you will need a far higher speed.

Most cameras will offer a shutter speed range of between 10 seconds and 1/1000th of a second.

Remember: Holding the camera will cause it to move or shake, even for a very short space of time. Shooting at speeds of about 1/60th of a second will compensate for this. Anything slower than this and you will need a tripod or a place to rest the camera such as a wall or chair.

This image was taken at 1/60th of a second as I wanted to capture the movement of the happy couple, the mad excitement and the roses being thrown

I needed a much higher shutter speed, than that of the image below, to 'freeze' the instant moment of this child's jump. It was shot at 1/1000th second

APERTURE

The aperture is the size of the hole through which the light passes. The size of the hole dictates the depth of field.

The aperture is described in 'f' stops, inversely in proportion to its size. A small or narrow aperture will give an image sharp focus from foreground to background, and is represented as a high number.

A large or wide aperture isolates the subject, with the background and foreground out-of-focus, and is represented by a low number.

For example, the camera would set a high 'f' stop (and therefore a narrow aperture) for a landscape, while you would desire a low 'f' stop (or a wide aperture) for portraits.

To highlight this bird against the bow of the boat I used a wide aperture – f2.8

For this scene, I wanted the boat, the bridge and the background all in focus so I needed a narrower aperture – f22

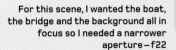

DEPTH OF FIELD

Depth of field influences the look of the picture enormously, but it is subjective because it depends on how you want the picture to look. Do you want everything to look crisp and sharp? Do you want to highlight the subject?

The control you have depends on the functions your camera offers but most will offer you a range of set 'portrait', 'landscape' and 'action' functions, if not the full manual option which allows you total control over the aperture and the shutter speed.

EXPOSURE

By combining the shutter speed and the aperture you get the exposure.

For example, when taking a portrait you might choose a wide aperture which would require you to use a fast shutter speed in order to limit the amount of light entering the camera. Conversely, if you chose a small aperture when photographing a landscape the shutter speed would need to be lower. You might even try to avoid camera shake by using a tripod.

You can usually see when a photograph isn't properly exposed. An underexposed image (see image 1) will look too dark while an overexposed image (see image 2) will look too bright.

A correctly exposed image is also dependent on the ISO (see page 21).

> Remember: The ISO dictates how sensitive the sensor is to light – this will obviously affect the exposure. On a bright sunny day you might want to choose a low sensitivity-to-light ISO, like 100 ISO (otherwise you might find that even at the fastest shutter speed the image is still overexposed at the widest aperture), while on a rainy, cloudy day you will probably choose something like 400 ISO.

2 Whereas here the shutter speed was too slow, allowing too much light into the camera, resulting in a washed-out look

1 Here, not enough light was allowed in to take a good photograph – the shutter speed was too quick

3 This image of commuters hurrying to work on a rainy day shows what a perfectly exposed image looks like. Compare it to images 1 and 2

However, remember that the higher the ISO the more graininess or 'noise' the image will have, which will affect the image quality. To what degree will depend on the quality and expense of your camera: more expensive models have pre-set functions on their mode dial, for example, which can really help you as you start out.

You can see from this picture of a boy in a church in Quito, Ecuador, how a high ISO affects the quality of an image. It was shot with a setting of 1600 ISO

MODE DIAL

As explained on page 21, the mode dial offers you the option of moving between different functions. As you get more confident with your camera, you will want to move on and take more control over your images. The different modes or functions will give you this increasing control.

M MANUAL

The settings are your call, depending on your requirements for the final look of the image. MANUAL allows manual adjustment of the aperture and the shutter speed.

A APERTURE PRIORITY

You set the aperture yourself depending on your preferences and the camera automatically sets the shutter speed to give the correct exposure.

S SHUTTER PRIORITY

You set the shutter speed yourself depending on your preferences and the camera will automatically set the aperture to give the correct exposure.

P PROGRAM

This is the same as AUTO but the camera will allow you to override the settings.

AUTO

Everything is set for you by the camera, from the shutter speed and aperture, to the use of flash. The camera makes these decisions by evaluating what is being focused on, the light available, etc.

DISPLAY IMAGES

Allows you to view your images and short movies.

SHORT FILM CAPACITY

Allows you to shoot short movies.

SCN SCENE SELECTION

PORTRAIT:

Wide aperture and faster shutter speed to isolate the subject.

LANDSCAPE:

Narrow aperture and slower shutter speed to keep both the foreground and background in focus.

ACTION:

Fast shutter speed with the aperture balanced depending on the amount of light available.

MACRO:

Wide aperture for close-up images.

ADDING IMPACT TO YOUR SHOTS

It doesn't take much to elevate your pictures to be more than just a record of an event. You can add drama, capture a look, record passion and emotion. We are surrounded by exciting possibilities every day and photographing them doesn't involve a great leap. We just need to train our 'eye' to see the potential around us. How often do our friends or relatives view the photographic record of our recent adventures with polite expressions and long-suffering airs, as we show them boring, lifeless prints? Let's make them say 'Wow!'.

The first thing you need to do is simply experiment. The joy of digital photography is that if you have a large enough memory card (or a couple as I have suggested), and batteries to back you up, you can take as many versions of the same thing as you want. Professional photographers call this working a subject – photographing it from many angles, trying things out until they are satisfied with the result.

When you are learning it is essential that you push the boundaries foward.

FOCUSING
Not everything has to be in focus. Sometimes by removing a sharp focus you are forced to see the basic shapes of things more clearly.

SHUTTER SPEEDS
Don't always freeze people in mid-action: use slower shutter speeds to show movement and blur. People don't always move at the same pace so it is important to be able to illustrate this in an image – think of a crowd of people moving at different speeds. Flash blur is a particularly interesting way of expressing movement – see page 45.

For this effect I wanted to capture the craziness of Christmas shopping so I used a slow shutter speed and a high aperture (1/5th of a second at f13) to expose the image correctly. I then chose my shopper and 'tracked' her as she walked up Oxford Street

Don't shoot everything you see from your head height; change depending on the subject but think about new angles to shoot from. For example, shoot low to the ground and see things from a child's point of view.

Sunset on the Houses of Parliament shot through a puddle (1/160th sec, f5)

For this shot of city workers after work I wanted to shoot from a low position to exaggerate their shapes against the bar, and remove as much of the distracting information from the lights of the bar as possible. With such low light I used a high ISO (1000 ISO) – even then I needed a wide aperture (f2.8) and a slow shutter speed (1/20th sec), plus a steady hand

For these two pictures (above and right) I thought the over-head shot would work the best – capturing the view of a pack of hounds gathered together and isolating the feet of a mother and daughter by a stream. But without a ladder handy I needed to hold the camera vertically above them without having the advantage of seeing exactly what I was shooting. It took a little trial and error but with digital cameras you have this luxury. They give you time to perfect the shot you want!

OVER/UNDEREXPOSURE

On some cameras you can set the exposure to shoot darker or brighter which can often bring some interesting results, as certain things get lost in the darkness or brightness and others become more highlighted.

AWARENESS OF SURROUNDINGS

A high level of awareness of your surroundings and situation is important. Try to be the 'all-seeing eye'; it is frustrating when an electricity pylon cuts straight across the scene, and you only 'see' it after you have taken the photograph.

Use the surroundings to take an 'interesting' picture!

For both of these shots (above and below) I was aiming to highlight the shape of the figures and therefore needed to expose for the light in the background. By placing the figures in front of the light you get the beautiful effect of the light radiating from the silhouettes. (Windsurfer: ISO 400, 1/160th sec, f5.6; Muse musician: ISO 400, 1/30th sec, f2.8)

Remember how important timing is. This was a quick glance upwards but perfect to capture this woman's reponse to the British weather

This not only goes for the physical things around us. We need to be aware of what is going to happen next – much of photography is about anticipating the moment. If it's a look somebody is about to make, the diving catch in a cricket match, the winning goal or just capturing a big, natural smile, the importance is in the moment – to anticipate and capture it.

It is also a good idea to see how other photographers work – wonderful images fill our newspapers and magazines every day and there are hundreds of exhibitions by world-renowned photographers. Take the time to see them and examine what you like about the images you see. Don't be afraid to copy the style of other photographers – all art students are sent to copy the Great Masters, so why shouldn't you do the same in your area of choice?

Photography requires a lot of patience as well. Robert Doisneau, the famous French photographer, waited for a whole day to capture his infamous picture *Le Regard Oblique* (Sidelong Glance) in 1948. While you may not have such a luxury, don't rush your pictures. Set the scene, compose it and then wait for the right moment. More often than not it will come.

The final thing to remember is to have confidence. It takes a while to be bold enough to photograph everything you see, often because you are worried about getting too close or upsetting people. The famous war photographer and founding member of Magnum Photos , Robert Capa, once said that if your photographs weren't good enough, you weren't close enough. And while this is not always the case, it is important to remember to get close enough to capture your image so that it is not just a dot in the middle of the frame.

COMPOSITION

Composition is about what goes where in an image. It is the bricks and mortar of a photograph. The strength, power and effect of a picture depends on its composition. Do we always position our subjects in the centre of the frame or is there any benefit in moving them to one side?

SOME RULES THAT CAN BE BROKEN

A number of traditional 'rules' are associated with composition and it is important that you learn them.

However, while it is useful to know these rules, it is even more important that you do not become a slave to them. Remember the value of experimenting and expressing what you see.

These two images show that there is real strength in not always framing your subject in the middle of the picture

1/3

1/3

The rule of thirds brings a wonderful sense of the size of the outdoors and sky, in both these images

GOLDEN MEAN

The 'rule of thirds' has been used as a means of composition strength by artists since its conception by the Greeks . If you divide the frame into three horizontal lines and three vertical lines and place your subject on these squares, the image becomes more engaging than simply always having the subject in the middle of the frame. Portraits often work better along the vertical lines, while landscapes often benefit by being arranged along horizontal lines.

SHAPES

Try half closing your eyes before you take a picture so everything is out of focus. You will see the shapes of things more clearly because they are not inhibited by the details which surround them. Which shapes work and why? What about the spaces between shapes – often called 'negative shapes'? Instead of focusing on, for example, the table and chair, look at the shapes between them. How these shapes work is very important to the strength of a composition.

And what about the basic shape or format of your image? Traditionally the horizontal shape is called 'landscape' whilst the vertical is called 'portrait', because these shapes lend themselves to these subjects. However, don't be constrained by this – think about the use of panoramic or 'letterbox' pictures for portraits: square shapes can be great too. While you won't be able to create these shapes at the camera stage (although some digital cameras have a 'panoramic' setting), you can easily create them later in your editing software by simply cropping the image (see page 57) . But think about it first and compose your image accordingly.

We can see how different shapes bring a different feel when we compare this panoramic river scene (opposite) and the portrait of writer Alan Bennett (above)

LINES

Allow the lines that make up our world to direct the eye towards or away from our subject. Pylons, roads, paths and trees can all be used to great effect.

Similarly, doorways, arches and even foliage can make good frames.

SYMMETRY

Symmetry makes an image feel solid and ordered. Look at the difference between the two images on this page.

Try thinking about the image before you raise your camera. Compose first, thinking about what you want to include and exclude and then bring the camera to your eye to make any fine adjustments with the zoom.

Invisible 'lines' can be created by people's direction of look; there are at least three such strong lines in the image below, taken during London's Pride festival in Soho

These surf boards lined up in a rack, and the three umbrellas opposite above, show how lines and symmetry help create an image with a very different feel to that of the more relaxed image from London's Pride festival, above right

PORTRAITS

I imagine the majority of us use our cameras to take pictures of the people around us – our friends and family – but how do we maximize the opportunities we have to capture that 'true' image of them?

One of the first things to consider is what focal length lens to use – remember, a wide-angle lens will distort the image slightly. Most digital cameras offer a 35mm equivalent lens which will produce some distortion. This will affect the appearance of your subject.

In a distorted image the lines will converge towards the outer edges of the frame, so anything placed within it will seem to bend. This can produce some interesting effects if that is what you are after – see the image below that illustrates this point.

This shot of photographers outside Buckingham Palace, shot with a 16mm lens, shows how the image has distorted due to using a wide-angled lens

This portrait of a performer at the Notting Hill Carnival, London, is also slightly distorted as it was shot with a 16mm lens

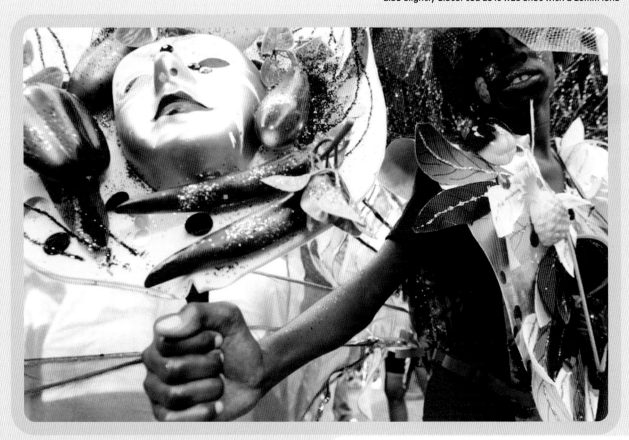

It is better, I feel, to use a longer focal length – not only will this avoid the trouble of distortion, it will create a shallower depth of field that will isolate and highlight the subject and also increase the distance between you and subject – many people, after all, resent having cameras pushed into their faces!

Try to set your focal length; I prefer to use 50mm equivalent and keep to it, using your feet rather than the zoom lens. Compose with your eyes rather than with the camera.

Secondly, is the image going to be posed or unposed?

If posed, remember to keep your subject/s entertained: try to avoid the 'firing line' look. Keep it quick but be confident in where you want them to be and what you want them to do. With single portraits I often find a prop is important – try to place something in the frame that is associated with what the person means to you, what they do or where they are. If photographing children, props will often prove to be a very necessary distraction. With group portraits, again try to move away from the police line-up shot and have some people standing, some sitting, etc. Force the viewer of the picture to 'move around' the image so that everyone is seen.

It was easy to shoot this picture of my two nieces as they chatted happily away: I was shooting with a long lens (110mm) on the other side of the river, which allowed them to relax so that I could capture a lovely moment between them

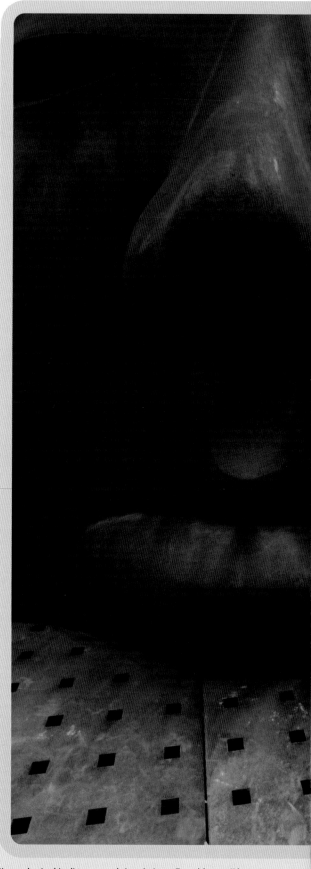

It was logical to line up sculptor Antony Donaldson with his sculpture of Alfred Hitchcock, firstly to show the scale but also to convey Hitchcock's importance. It was shot on a wide-angle 17mm lens to exaggerate the scale

I often find that taking a second picture immediately after the first one works well. People are prepared for the first shot – they have their 'photography face' on – and the resulting image can look wooden and unreal. However, they won't be expecting the second exposure, so they will look more natural, having relaxed a bit.

If the photo is unposed, then anticipation is the most important thing. Be patient and prepared as the right moment can come in the blink of an eye. Have the camera ready, with the correct settings prepared, ready to pounce!

Patience and timing were used to great effect to catch this wonderful moment backstage at the National Festival of Music for Youth, at the Royal Festival Hall, London

Remember: There will be shutter lag or delay between pressing the shutter button and the picture being captured (how much depends on your individual camera) – so try to snap just as your subject is about to laugh, for example, to capture their full smile.

LIGHTING

Lighting is an important constituent of all types of photography, including portraits. Remember that as a photographer your goal is to 'paint with light'. Think about where the light is coming from – don't always go for the traditional shot with the sun behind you.

Contre-jour ('against the light') shots will create a sometimes desirable 'halo-effect': light from the side will give you nice, long shadows; direct light on a bright sunny day will cause your subject to squint and deep shadows or 'panda-eyes' will be created, so diffused or softer light is better – try using the light that comes from windows or from a doorway.

Shooting into the light and behind this person relaxing in a London park gave me an interesting silhouette as well as conveying the haziness and heat of the day

I was able to capture this picture at a fashion show by allowing the light behind the model to creep to one side, giving the viewer the shape of the woman but also the interesting rainbow flare created as the direct light hit my lens

For this portrait, lit from the side by the harsh daylight from a window, the dark background also allowed me to catch the train and a puff of steam

Try, if possible, to use natural light and avoid the use of the flash (see below). If necessary increase the ISO level to achieve the desired result.

Home-made reflectors (silver-foil wrapped around a tray, for example) will allow you to lighten up a dark area by reflecting or bouncing light from a source such as a window.

When considering the light, remember to recognize the kind of light falling on your subject. Different light has different tones. For example, the light from a lamp is much warmer than light on a cloudy day. What you need to do is find the 'true' white of your light source. Unlike a conventional camera, in which you need to replace the film each time the light changes, the white balance function in your digital camera can be adjusted for different types of light. Often the auto white balance – usually one of the many default settings on your camera (see page 21) – will do this for you but most cameras will offer you the chance to change it manually to have more control.

FLASH PHOTOGRAPHY
Virtually all modern compact digital cameras will have an in-built flash. The default settings on your camera will turn to auto flash but, while it is useful, it is not very subtle. Flash can cause some horrendous-looking results: washed-out faces, red-eye and flat or ill-lit backgrounds. I would propose getting to grips with the manual settings of your flash as soon as possible.

Remember: Be careful when taking pictures in mixed or competing light sources. A sitting room, for example, with light from the window, light from a table-lamp and light from an overhead ceiling lamp can create three different shades of colour. In my experience it is better to choose the light which is lighting the subject manually or, if there is no subject, the light which is most dominant. Any further variations can be corrected in your editing software later on and will be covered in Chapter Five

The flash on your camera normally fires at 1/60 second. By using the manual settings you can select a shutter speed of 1/10 second, for example, which will enable more natural light to register. You can also avoid washed-out faces by turning the power of the flash down and standing further away from your subject.

As mentioned above, try using natural light where possible, but on bright sunny days use the flash to compensate for dark shadows. This is called 'fill-in' flash: it can be a little hard to get used to the idea of using the flash when you seem to have plenty of light, but it is a very useful trick to know about.

Experimentation is key; remember there's no film to waste!

This image of a rather bizarre al fresco hairdresser needed flash to light the artists and keep the background of blue sky and clouds correctly exposed

LANDSCAPES AND CITYSCAPES

The world around us, in both its natural landscapes and its man-made cityscapes, provides excellent opportunities for photographs.

Cityscapes can be very interesting, especially at night or at dusk when the sky is still light but the city lights have come on. You will definitely need a tripod for this kind of shot.

Don't forget that much of the interest in photographing architecture is in the detail – examine the shapes and angles of particular buildings and how they interact with other buildings around them.

PANORAMAS

Many cameras will offer you a panoramic setting. This is a bit of a con because what they actually do is just chop the top and bottom off the original frame. Perfect if you don't have a computer on which to edit your images, and very simply done if you do have one. Creating a panorama will be covered later (see page 62) but set the camera manually when taking a photograph in this format because the light can change dramatically between shade and brighter areas as you move.

Remember: Keep a narrow aperture – this may force you to use a tripod but they can be very inexpensive, especially if your camera is small and lightweight. Choose the shortest focal length possible, be patient and wait for the right light – traditionally dawn and dusk can provide stunning images of landscapes but similarly cloudy days can produce some dramatic results.

For both these pictures the clouds with the sunlight coming through them are what provides the dramatic effect (Wembley: ISO 250, 1/500th sec, f11; Other: ISO 200, 1/2000th sec, f8)

COLOUR

COLOUR VS. BLACK AND WHITE

One of the real perks of digital photography is that it allows us to shoot in both colour and black and white – no changing of film: just push a button and there it goes. I would, however, urge against using the 'monochrome' setting that many digital cameras offer. It can be helpful to see what a black and white image will look like, and because it is only using one colour it needs much less information and therefore less memory space to store it. Unless this is a major concern (you may find you only have a small amount left on your memory card) I would tend to use the camera's maximum-quality setting and the most data possible – remember, it is always better to have more quality and risk memory card space, than to be unable to use a nice image after all because you find you need more 'information' to edit it as you wish.

When taking an image that you want to develop as a black and white image, remember that instead of being concerned with colour you need to be more aware of everything else: the shapes, the expressions, the light, the contrast, the emotion. Try and see in black and white, and look for the light and shade, the shadows and the highlights.

The power of this art installation in central London is helped by the small figure in red at the bottom

This shot of an audience at a concert in Barcelona, Spain, was taken in colour but to make it work better it was converted to black and white

USING COLOUR

How you can change a colour image into a black and white image will be discussed on pages 81-83.
While it is true that taking black and white images requires us to concentrate on other factors, taking photos in colour requires us to concentrate on the colours we are including in our image. Colour, as a tool for composition, can help us make more of an impact with our pictures. For example, instead of shooting a single scene with a mass of colours, try focusing on the contrast between two or three colours, ignoring the subject completely. Make the colour your subject.

This cloud scene shows a great depth of different colours, and works despite it being simply a quick snapshot of clouds

MOVEMENT

SILHOUETTES

The stationary, moment-in-time shape of silhouettes highlight the contrast between the blacked-out shapes of buildings or people, and the colour of the sky or wall (for example) behind the subject. The key here is to expose (set the shutter speed) for the background and then focus on the darker foreground shape of the silhouette.

Silhouettes are a great way of using light to your advantage by emphasizing shape and emotion. This image of Tai Chi needed this type of light manipulation to add serenity to the scene

ACTION AND SPORTS

The key here is anticipation and a fast shutter speed. You will need to be able to predict what is going to happen next, compensate for the delay in your shutter and then freeze your subject.

This indoor windsurfing competition required great anticipation as the light was low and the boards were moving very quickly

CREATING A BLURRED EFFECT

There are a few tricks you can learn which will add to the effect of movement. The simplest is just to slow the shutter speed down to create a blurred effect – a tripod is useful to keep the background sharp. 'Panning' is when you keep your moving subject sharp whilst the background appears to be moving: you achieve this by slowing the shutter speed down as far as you can while avoiding camera shake as you follow the moving subject (or pan) with your camera, pressing the shutter button down in the middle of this tracking motion.

Try experimenting with a moving car or jogger – the closer you are to the subject the greater the effect will be.

Another trick is when you keep the camera very still, preferably on a tripod, select a slow shutter speed of around 1/8th second (depending on how fast the subject is moving) and keep the flash turned on. This is called 'flash blur' and can be great to express movement. It works especially well when the subject is moving from one side of the frame to the other.

This car competition offered the chance to show the speed the cars were travelling at. One flash at a slow shutter speed will create the effect of 'flash blur'

FROM CAMERA TO COMPUTER

You are now at the next and perhaps most exciting stage of the digital process. No longer do you have to deal with smelly and messy chemicals cluttering up your home – all you need is access to a computer and a little time.

If you don't have a computer there are many places along the high street which will cheaply and effectively develop your pictures. They should give you a CD that contains all the images, in their original form, so you can always come back to them at a later date. Take care of these CDs because they are the 'negatives' of this digital age.

4.0 FROM CAMERA TO COMPUTER

CHOICE OF COMPUTER

There are two main types of computer – the PC or the Apple Macintosh (commonly known as a Mac). By far the most popular are PCs. The difference is that PCs are made by many different manufacturers, but happily most use Microsoft Windows as their operating system. Put simply the PC is just the body: the operating system the brain.

Macs, on the other hand, are only made by Apple and as such have their own operating system, known as OS.

You will need to check that your camera is compatible with the computer you have. Most cameras are compatible with all types but it is worth checking if you have an old, or brand-new, computer.

The choice between the two is very subjective. PCs are cheaper than their Mac equivalents because of the competition between manufacturers. It is worth taking advice on this when you come to buy a computer, or update your old one.

DOWNLOADING TO YOUR COMPUTER

BEFORE YOU START
There are two ways to 'download' or copy your images onto your computer.

FROM YOUR CAMERA
All digital cameras come with a lead. This is usually a USB (universal serial bus) cable which is the universal method of attaching an external device such as a camera to a PC or Mac. More advanced cameras will come with a 'Firewire' lead which is more expensive but quicker. The first and most important thing is to make sure that your computer is compatible with these leads. Most modern computers will have USB sockets but some might not have Firewire as yet. Happily, adapters can be bought if you find they are not compatible.

When the camera is attached, an icon should appear on your desktop, as well as Microsoft's (PC users) Picture Package. You will be offered a choice of options from downloading to slideshows.

You should then click on the option to Download.

> Remember: Each camera will come with its own software package. It is important to download and read it carefully. If you have any queries, each software package will have a 'read me' section which should help. This will allow your computer to successfully 'read' your camera when attached.

FROM YOUR CARD READER

One of the disadvantages of downloading from your camera is that it uses up a lot of battery power. One way around this is to buy a card reader – these vary in terms of price, speed and USB vs. Firewire compatibility, but they can be very useful because they can be permanently connected to the computer. This saves you the trouble of connecting your camera to your computer every time you want to download.

Most digital cameras do not come with a card reader but they are easy to find in any high street electrical store.

When attached, the card reader's icon should appear on your desktop.

Once the icon appears on your computer's desktop, you need to open the folder by double-clicking on the icon. This will open up whatever images you have taken. From here you will need to copy all the images from the icon to one of your folders.

FILING

Perhaps one of the most important aspects to consider, especially if you are not too familiar with computers, is to have an organized filing system. If you think of your computer as an electronic filing cabinet with drawers, folders and sub-folders and files inside these folders it will be easier to organize yourself.

Most software, be it camera or computer, will want to download your images into the My Pictures folder (for PC and Microsoft Windows users). But you should also have the chance to create a new folder that you can call whatever you choose. If, under your My Pictures folder, you keep other sub-folders such as Family, Summer Holiday or Christening, for example, you will not only be able to find your images more quickly but, more importantly, they won't get lost in the depths of your computer.

A QUICK EDIT

The simple software package that comes with your computer or with your camera will offer you the chance to have a quick look at your pictures. This will be the first time you will have seen them – which should be very exciting.

This is also the moment to delete and copy some of your images. I would suggest that those images you know you love and want to keep should be copied and saved in another file, or on a back-up disc for added safety. This also means that if there are any problems when you come to editing them later, you will have another copy elsewhere. Also, even if you have been very conservative with your shooting, there will probably be some images that are not worth keeping and it is at this stage that you can delete them.

However, it is worth remembering that images that are under or overexposed or horribly out-of-focus can produce some funky and surreal images with enough playing around in your editing software. You may also find that an area, such as a section of sky can be removed from a dud image and placed on another to make it even better.

> **Remember: Save your image as a duplicate image before editing in case anything goes wrong and you lose the original. And be careful, because once you delete, you delete forever (although even this is not strictly true: see page 22).**

THE EDITING PROCESS

This is the moment when you bring the darkroom into your living room, leave the chemicals behind and, perhaps for the first time, take complete control of your own images.

From now on you don't have to risk the possibility of the high street processors messing up your images and leaving them bland and pale. By being in charge of their treatment yourself you can turn your images into works of art.

5.0 THE EDITING PROCESS

CALIBRATING YOUR MONITOR

Before you start to edit, calibrating your monitor is vital – it ensures that the colours are correct and that you are using the right amount of brightness and contrast, as well as giving your software a profile to work from. It will also help once you are in a position to print because the profile will create some consistency between the image you see on the monitor and that produced by the printer.

Most monitors will arrive with a default setting but it is useful to make sure. Once Photoshop Elements is open check that the background is a neutral grey colour. Even if it is, it is worth checking that your monitor has been fully calibrated.

Make sure your Photoshop Elements has been installed.

1   Leave your monitor on for thirty minutes (this warms up the colours)
2   click on the Windows **Start** button
3   click on the **Control Panel**
4   double-click on the **Adobe Gamma** icon
5   click on **Step by Step** for the Windows Wizard to take you through the settings.

Remember: There are certain things you need to check before you buy software such as if it has a compatible operating system: i.e. does it work on both Windows and Mac? What amount of hard disc space (memory issues) and RAM (this dictates the speed of the processor and how quickly software will operate) does your choice of software require?

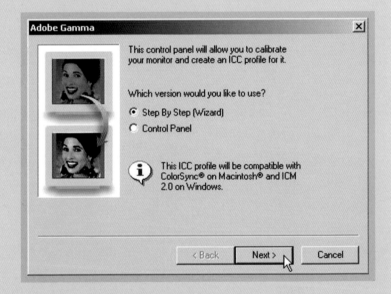

YOUR SOFTWARE CHOICES

Although you will be using Photoshop Elements it is important that you know and understand the alternative software options.

ADOBE PHOTOSHOP
This is, in my opinion, the best choice to go for if you are at all serious about editing your images. Though more expensive than its rivals, it offers the most in terms of versatility and power.

ADOBE PHOTOSHOP ELEMENTS
This is the simplified version of the above and the one you will be using in this book. It is cheaper and great for starting out but you may find yourself limited when you get more familiar with using it.

JASC PAINTSHOP PRO
This is a very popular editing program aimed at the amateur, consumer market. It is cheaper than Photoshop but it is only compatible with Windows.

THE GIMP
This is one of the few free editing suites and is compatible with both Windows and Mac. A good start if you are unsure and want somewhere to start out.

ROXIO PHOTOSUITE
This is aimed at the sporadic user and as such doesn't do a great deal.

FILE TYPES

As you saw in Chapter Two, once you have taken an image all the data information such as colour, shapes and contrast is interpreted by the processor inside the camera and then saved as a file onto the memory card. Similarly, once you have opened up an image in your editing software and made various changes, you then need to save your image as a particular file.

There are many different file types offering their own advantages and disadvantages, but you only really need to know about a few:

JPEG (JOINT PHOTOGRAPHIC EXPERT GROUP; .JPG)
This is the most common and universally compatible file type. It is used in nearly all the digital cameras in the market place. This is because it compresses, or packs in, more data which means you get more shots. It gives you control over the size and quality of your image, allowing high settings for your printing needs and lower ones for sending over the internet or your mobile phone. The only thing you need to be aware of is that opening the same JPEG file on your computer more than four or five times will reduce its quality.

RAW (CAMERA RAW; .CRW)
This is the other major file type used in cameras. Mostly found in SLRs and the more expensive compact cameras, RAW files offer the advantage of holding the maximum amount of information but at the disadvantage of much larger file sizes. This means, of course, that you are able to take fewer images on your memory card than when saving as JPEGs. Unless you have the latest Photoshop, using RAW files will also force you into using your camera's own particular brand of software to open and edit them.

TIFF (TAG IMAGE FILE FORMAT; .TIF)
Only a few cameras offer TIFF files but most editing software automatically chooses the best choice for printing and saving your work. Although they use much larger files than JPEGs and even RAW files, they are easy to compress (which means you can reduce their size to send them quickly over the internet), with no reduction in quality. I would suggest you save all your favourite images as TIFF files.

PHOTOSHOP (.PSD)
Particular to the editing software. Much the same as TIFFs but it does suffer from compatibility problems if the person you send your image to doesn't have Photoshop.

GIF (GRAPHIC INTERCHANGE FORMAT; .GIF)
Though not great for images because of the reduced number of colours it uses, it can be useful if you just want to send images via your mobile phone.

THE TOOLBAR AND PHOTOSHOP ELEMENTS SCREEN

In this book you will be using Photoshop Elements 3 to take you through the various editing procedures. Don't worry if you have another type because many of the tools and operations are typical of most editing software.

The first thing to get to grips with is the **Toolbar** where you will start to make the adjustments needed to turn your images into the perfect pictures you've always wanted.

The toolbar offers you three main areas of editing: the **Selection** of parts of the image; the **Image Correction** tools, for tasks such as making images lighter or darker; and finally the **Brush** tools: for example, paintbrushes or text pencils. If you press one of the short-cut letters (seen here in bold) on your keyboard, you can move quickly around the toolbar and the choices within each. If you hold your cursor over the individual tool, its name will pop up.

TOOLBAR

1. MOVE TOOL **V**
Enables you to move a selection or layer

2. ZOOM TOOL **Z**
This enlarges and reduces the image view and can be used to select a specific area to view

3. HAND TOOL **H**
Enables you to move around an image. Very useful when working on detailed parts

4. EYEDROPPER TOOL **I**
Allows you to choose the foreground and background colours

5. MARQUEE TOOLS **M**
Used to select shapes inside your image to edit without affecting the rest of the image

6. LASSO TOOL **L**
Allows you to make your own shaped selection by drawing around an image

7. MAGIC WAND TOOL **W**
Selects pixels of a similar colour – the degree of this can be easily adjusted

8. SELECTION BRUSH TOOL **A**
Allows you to draw an area – gives you more flexibility than the marquee tools

9. TEXT TOOL **T**
Enables you to write on your images

10. CROP **C**
Deletes the area outside the selected shape

11. COOKIE CUTTER TOOL **Q**
Allows you to crop an image with one of the given shapes e.g. a heart

12. RED-EYE REMOVAL TOOL **Y**
Removes the red-eye effect caused by direct flash hitting the retina

13. SPOT HEALING BRUSH TOOL **J**
Removes dust and other imperfections on your image as well as whole objects

14. CLONE STAMP TOOL **S**
This tool copies pixels from one area and pastes them onto another

15. PENCIL TOOL **N**
Paints onto the image with its size and shape easily adjusted

16. ERASER **E**
Offers the chance to remove pixels using either a pencil, brush or block

17. BRUSH TOOL **B**
Paints onto the image with its size and shape easily adjusted

18. PAINT BUCKET TOOL **K**
Fills a selected area with a given colour

19. GRADIENT TOOL **G**
Blends one colour into another – great for smooth backgrounds

20. SHAPE SELECTION TOOL **U**
Creates pre-defined custom shapes

21. BLUR AND SHARPEN TOOL **R**
Softens or sharpens pixels

22. DODGE, BURN AND SPONGE TOOL **O**
Lightens, darkens and de-saturates areas

23. FOREGROUND AND BACKGROUND COLORS OR SWATCHES
Allows you to select foreground and background colour

The whole toolbar can be moved around your desktop by clicking and holding down on the six dots at the top and dragging your mouse.

SETTING UP PHOTOSHOP ELEMENTS

Before you begin to edit your pictures it is important that you set the correct colour for what you want to do with your image.

1 Go to Photoshop Elements
2 click on **Colour Settings** (window 1)
3 click on **Full Colour Management** if you are working on images to print, or click on **No Colour Management** to leave as the default settings (window 2)
4 click **OK**
5 when saving your images remember to make sure **ICC Profiles** (Windows) or **Embed Colour Profile** (Mac OS) is ticked.

window 1

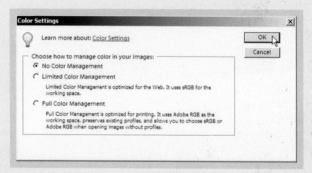

window 2

OPENING AN IMAGE

Once you have become acquainted with the toolbar and the look of your editing software you are ready to start doing your own editing.

1 Open up your editing software by double-clicking the icon.
> once Photoshop Elements is open you need to make sure you have the correct windows or toolbars open. At the top bar, where it says Photoshop Elements there will be a row of tools starting with **File** down to **Help**.
2 click on **File** and move along the toolbar with your mouse – as you do options will open up below for each. (Those in bold will be ones you can use – obviously more will be available once you have an image open.)

3 click on **Windows** and make sure that both the options **Tools** and **Tool Options** are ticked. If they are not, click on them once with your mouse.
> on the left will be your **Toolbar** as described in the last chapter. Above will be your **Tool Options** bar giving you the various choices for each tool. If you take a moment to look at how two different tools look it will give you an idea of how they all work.
4 click on the **Text** tool or press **T** on your keyboard. By moving your mouse slowly along the **Tool Options** bar you will see what options you have at your fingertips: horizontal to vertical writing, the different style fonts, bold or unbold, the size of the font, the colour, etc.

Now let's open an image.

1 Click on **File**
2 click on **Browse Folders** (window 1)
> the top left smaller window entitled **Folders** gives you the chance to navigate through your files and folders. If you click on, for example, **My Pictures** all the files in that folder will open up (window 2)
3 click on one of the images and a thumbnail (a small version of the image) in the second box will appear in the box entitled **Preview**
> below this box is a box entitled **Metadata** and **Keywords**. In **Metadata** you can view the various bits of information such as the date it was taken, the file type it was shot on, the file size and other data. In the keywords section you can allocate words which will in the future help you locate these files, such as where they were taken.

At the top of the small **Folders** box you are given further options. If you move your mouse onto **File** you will see how you have the chance to open and delete images: **Edit** allows you to perform simple tasks such as rotating the image; **Automate** gives you the chance to create slideshows and montages; **Sort** orders the files shown depending on date or file name or size; finally **View** is how and what you see, all the files or only some, from a small or a large thumbnail.

You can set all these choices or preferences depending on what suits you best.

The ability of **View** to see all the images at a glance is a wonderful way of choosing which image you want to work on. Some other types of editing software will force you to open the image up completely before seeing it – which is obviously not as good.

Once you have chosen an image you want to start working on, you can either:

1 Double-click the thumbnail in the **Preview** box
2 double-click the image in the right hand box with all the other images or go to **File** and **Open** at the top of the **File Browser** box (window 3).

There are many ways to choose from, but for me double-clicking the image you want is the easiest. All the options at the top should now be highlighted, indicating that you can now use them.

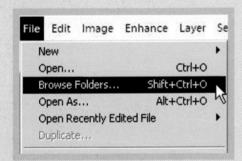

window 1

window 2

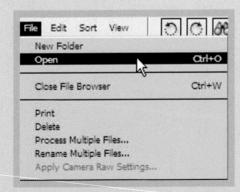

window 3

STRAIGHTENING AND CROPPING

One of the huge advantages of digital images is the ease with which you can crop and shape the image you have taken. Though purists might shudder, the crop tool has a number of important roles:

window 4

> it allows you to remove distractions that take away from the main subject
> you can change a horizontal image to a vertical image, and vice versa
> you can use other shapes rather than the traditional horizontal and vertical shapes
> it straightens up an unaligned image.

In this example we'll see how you can successfully remove distractions to make an image bolder and the subject stand out.

1 **Open** your image
2 click on the **Crop Tool** (window 4)
3 click and hold down the mouse button and drag it over the image you want to keep
4 use the 8 handle-points around the cropped part to make fine adjustments
5 use the corners to tilt the image as required (window 5)
6 once you are happy, click the **Return** button (window 6)
7 to save your new image click on **File** and then **Save As**.

window 5

window 6

SAVING A FILE

It is important to know how to save a file successfully.

Clicking on the **Save As** box (window 1) will offer you three choices:
- what name to give your new file
- where to place it
- what file type to choose.

If you save it as a **JPEG** (window 2) another box will appear. This gives you the chance to dictate the quality of the file from low to high levels on a scale of 1 – 12.
> for printing you want as high a quality as possible, so select 12 (window 3).

If you are saving any other file types, such as TIFF or Photoshop, it is safe just to use the default settings.

window 1

window 3

window 2

SAVING FILES FOR EMAILS OR PHONES

A lot of the pleasure in using digital cameras comes from the ease of sharing pictures with our friends amd family by using email and photo messaging. However, if you are taking your photographs on the highest quality setting (which I suggest you do) you might find it more convenient to reduce the image size otherwise the file will be very large and will take a long time to send and then open at the other end.

As we have seen, the size of an image is dictated by the number of pixels along the image's height and width. This shows how much information or 'image data' is stored in the image. The quality of an image is dictated by the resolution measure in pixels per inch (ppi) – the more pixels the better the quality.

We will cover this topic again, in greater detail, when we look at printing our images (see page 91).

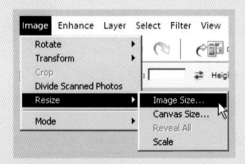

window 4

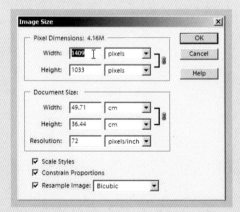

window 5

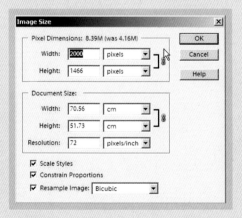

window 6

THE FIRST WAY OF CHANGING THE SIZE
Once you have edited your image:

1 Click on **Image**
2 click on **Resize** (window 4)
3 click on **Image Size**
4 make sure the **Constrain Proportions** box is ticked
> you can adjust the size of the image by adjusting the **Pixel Dimensions** and you will see how the height will change automatically as you change the width (windows 5 and 6)
> you can also change the image size by altering the **Document Size** in the same way
> for emailing I would keep the **Resolution** at 72 ppi (for printing this can be increased up to 300ppi)
> at the top of the box the **Pixel Dimensions** will show you the size of your image compared to what it was.

The disadvantage of this is that it requires some trial and error to get the right size, especially when dealing with emails.

THE SECOND WAY OF CHANGING THE SIZE
Another way is using the **Save For Web** mode.

1 Go to **File** (window 1)
2 a box will appear showing how the image will appear if you send it unaltered. The first box (under the **Help** option) dictates the quality of your image: I would suggest using the highest quality
3 click on **JPEG** in the first box and **High** in the second (window 2). If you are only sending examples or you have a slow modem you can easily reduce these settings
4 the next box will show you the image's **Original Size**

5 the next box allows you to alter the size (window 3). Make sure the **Constrain Proportions** is ticked and then adjust the **Resize Potential**
6 then click on **Apply** (window 4) and watch the image change to show how it will appear on screen
7 if you are happy click on **OK**
8 and then **Save As** and decide what the file is to be called, and where you want it saved to
9 finally, click on **Save**.

> Remember: Any measurement that you increase will also increase the file size.

window 1

window 2

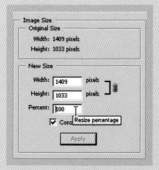

window 3

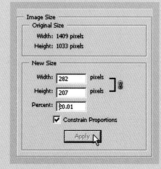

window 4

CHANGING THE SHAPE OF YOUR IMAGE

Changing the shape of your image is another useful function of the **Crop Tool**. Quite often, when you look at an image you see that it might work better horizontally or vertically.

Some digital cameras offer a panoramic option –this is slightly confusing because it implies the ability to see more than on the normal settings. In fact all it does is delete the top and bottom section of the image, giving the impression of a wider shot. This is easily achieved in Photoshop Elements.

By following the same steps as above you can crop the top and bottom of your image to create a panoramic or 'letterbox' shape. In the following pages you will discover how to 'stitch' two or more images together to create an even wider panoramic, but for now this is the easiest way to achieve it with a certain degree of control.

window 5

window 6

The **Crop Tool** allows us to create other shapes. The square shape is very popular (because it is the shape used by the professional medium format cameras), especially for portraits.

Another way to create funnier, more informal shapes is by using the **Cookie Cutter** tool.

1   Open an image
2   click on the **Cookie Cutter** tool
3   move your mouse up to the **Tool Options** bar
4   click on the **Shape** box (window 6) and select the shape you wish to use
5   click and drag on the image itself and the shape will emerge
>   you can make fine adjustments by using the handles on the edge
>   you can move the image by holding the mouse button down and dragging the centre spot to where you want to position the crop
6   once you are happy click on **Return**
7   click on **File** and then **Save As**.

> Remember: When you crop to such a degree you are effectively halving the size/amount of pixels of the image which will therefore affect the size to which the image can be printed whilst maintaining the same quality.

IMAGE STITCHING FOR PANORAMAS

In order to create a proper panorama you have to combine several images into one continuous image. The **Photomerge Panorama** command allows us to do this.

THINGS TO CONSIDER BEFORE TAKING A PANORAMA

> try to make sure your images overlap by more than 20 per cent. This will allow the software sufficient room to organize the images automatically
> use the same focal length in order to keep the perspective the same
> maintain the same exposure by using the manual settings
> try using a tripod to keep the image level.

CREATING A PANORAMA

1   Click on **File**
2   click on **New** (window 1)
3   click on **Photomerge Panorama** (window 2)
4   using the **Browse** option select the images you want to use for your panorama

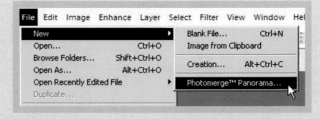

window 1

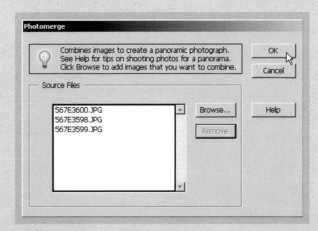

window 2

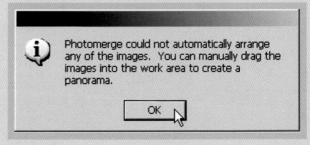

window 3

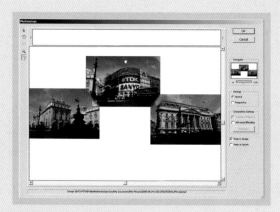

window 4

window 5

5   once you have selected them click on **OK** (window 3)

6   wait while the software creates new layers for your images

\>   if the images are closely aligned your panorama will automatically appear. If not, the images will appear in the **Lightbox** where you can manually drag the images into the **Work Area** (window 4) and match them as you see fit (window 5)

\>   to navigate around use the **Hand** tool

\>   use the **Zoom** tool or slider to enlarge or expand your image on screen.

CHANGING THE PERSPECTIVE

1   Select **Perspective** in the settings area

2   select the **Vanishing Point** tool and click on the area you want (usually the centre point)

3   finally, make sure that **Advanced Blending** is ticked in the **Composition Settings** to make sure the colour is similar all the way through (window 6).

window 6

IMPROVING YOUR IMAGES

It is a common problem to come home from the processors and be disappointed with the dull colours and lack of impact in our pictures. Often, many of them bear no resemblance to the wonderful colours and strength we saw in the original scene. This dull look can often be blamed on a lack of contrast: the difference between the light tones and the dark tones in the image.

Of course a lack of contrast occurs initially if you take a picture in a light where there is little difference between the dark areas and the light areas. This produces a 'flat' look without much impact. But even so, many processors, especially the cheaper high street ones, are unable to reproduce the contrast in your images.

This is where our digital editing software comes into such great use. There are two ways to achieve better contrast in your images:

1   Open your image
2   go to **Enhance**
3   click on **Auto Contrast** (window 1).

This leaves the decision up to the software and while this is certainly the easiest way, it doesn't offer much control. I would suggest trying it first and if you are not happy you can easily undo what you've done:

1   Click on **Edit**
2   click on **Undo Adjust Auto Contrast**
3   click on **Enhance**
4   click on **Adjust Lighting**
5   click on **Brightness/Contrast** (window 2)
6   once it's open make sure the **Preview** button is checked
>   adjust using the slider until you are happy (window 3).

I think that pushing the contrast above 14 or 15 takes away too much from the image. However, the decision is yours.

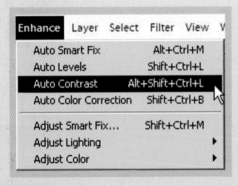

window 1

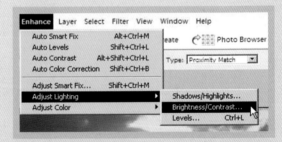

window 2

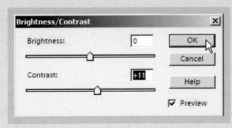

window 3

Photoshop Elements also has a clever and very easy system to enhance your images which you can take a look at now.

In the top right hand corner of your window you will see a choice between **Standard Edit** and **Quick Fix**. While I suggest staying with **Standard Edit**, to save time and effort the **Quick Fix** tool can be very useful.

Click on it now and you will see various windows appear automatically. You will now have the chance to make some of the most basic adjustments you will need to edit your pictures.

In our present example (window 4) you now have the opportunity to change the contrast using **Midtone**

Contrast – this will affect the tones that are half way between pure white and pure black. You can also rotate the image and change the overall lighting and colour, the hue and saturation and the definition or sharpness.

At the bottom left of your window you will see a little box titled **View** which offers different choices of view while you make your changes.

AFTER ONLY	shows the changes as you make them
BEFORE ONLY	shows the original image
BEFORE AND AFTER	(portrait) comparison of the changes displayed vertically
BEFORE AND AFTER	(landscape) comparison of the changes displayed horizontally.

window 4

ADJUSTING THE HUE AND SATURATION

The Hue/Saturation command adjusts the hue (the colour itself), saturation (strength of the colour) and the lightness of the whole image or of an individual colour.

Adding more saturation is another great way of adding punch to your images. The saturation of colours is essentially the essence and strength of the colour. The more saturated a colour is, the less grey it contains. Below you can see the difference saturated colours make to our colour images:

Standard Edit mode

1 Click on **Enhance**
2 click on **Adjust Color** (window 1)
3 click on **Adjust Hue/Saturation**
> make sure the **Edit** box says **Master**
4 click on and drag the sliders on the **Saturation** line to increase or decrease the strength of all the colours (window 2)
> if you simply want to adjust a single colour, click on **Edit** in the top left hand corner of the box and choose one of the colours (window 3)
5 again hold down and drag the sliders of the **Saturation** line to adjust the strength of that particular colour.

If you choose an individual colour, the adjustment slider becomes available – this allows you to widen or narrow the range of colours that is affected by the hue, saturation or lightness controls.

Try to avoid using the **Lightness** slider because this affects the overall tone of the image. This operation can be better achieved using other methods.

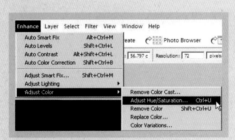

window 1

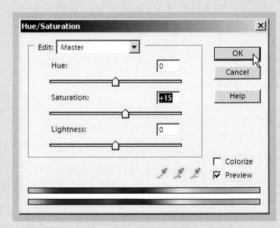

window 2

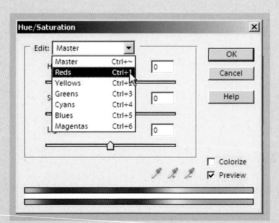

window 3

Working in the **Quick Edit** mode gives you the chance to adjust both the hue and the saturation but only the overall colours – it doesn't allow you to select an individual colour.

This box also allows you to adjust the **Hue**. Hue is our perception of colour – basically what you see as red, yellow or green. By using the sliders in the same way as I have described on the previous page, you can change the existing colours. For example, if you look at this image of an art installation in London's Trafalgar Square you can see how the yellow of the bananas can be changed quite dramatically.

window 4

SELECTING AN AREA INSIDE YOUR IMAGE

Now that you have seen how to add impact to your images by improving the contrast and saturation, it would be good to show you how we can select parts of images, enabling us to isolate and edit without affecting the rest of the image.

This is an invaluable part of the process because later on you will see how you can lighten, darken and make other adjustments to small sections of your images.

You can select different areas in a number of different ways.

TO SELECT A REGULAR SHAPE:

1   Click on the **Marquee** tool or press **M** on your keyboard
>   by pressing **M** you can alternate between a rectangular or elliptical shape. Alternatively, you can move your mouse pointer to the top of the **Tool Options** bar (window 5)
2   make sure the first of the four **Selection** boxes is checked
>   you can move the area selected with your mouse.

If you need to add on or remove sections of your shape move your mouse to one of the **Selection** boxes and click on, for example, **Add To Selection**.

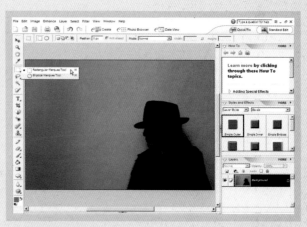

window 5

3   Hold and drag your mouse again and another shape will be attached
>   if you are unhappy and want to start again simply click off the selected shape
>   once you are happy with the positioning of your shape you can begin to make the colour, contrast or other adjustments just to that area.

FEATHERING

An important option found in the **Tool Options** bar is the **Feather** control: this allows you to smooth the hard edges of a selection and blurs the difference between the selected and unselected areas (window 1). This gradual change or transition means you can work on selected areas without making your changes too obvious.

Trial and error is the best way to achieve the best results, and the correct amount of feather depends on the original image and the degree of changes you want to make.

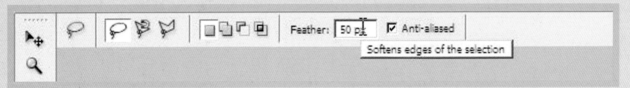

window 1

TO MAKE AN IRREGULAR SHAPE

More often than not the shape you want to edit is going to be irregular – for example, the face of the person in your portrait – but Photoshop Elements provides the appropriate tool.

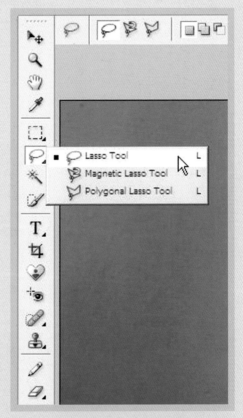

If you are working on a small, detailed area it is always wise to zoom in on the area ready for selection.

1   Click on the **Zoom** tool
>   use **Shift** and **+** together to zoom in or, for more control, hold and drag the mouse pointer to the area you want to select
3   click on the **Lasso Tool** or press **L** on your keyboard
>   by pressing **L** you can shift between the normal **Lasso Tool** (allows you to draw a freehand selection), the **Magnetic Lasso Tool** (automatically attaches itself to edges, making it quick and easy to make precise selections) and the **Polygonal Lasso Tool** (uses straight-lined selections) (window 2). Otherwise, simply move your mouse pointer up to the top right of the **Tool Options** bar
4   hold and drag your mouse pointer around the area you wish to select (with both the **Magnetic** and **Polygonal Lasso** tools you don't need to hold down, just click and move the mouse)
>   if you make an error you don't need to start all over again. Simply press **Delete** and you will go back a step.

If you need to add on or remove sections of your shape:

1   Move your mouse pointer to one of the **Selection** boxes
2   click on, for example, **Add To Selection**
3   click and drag your mouse pointer again and another shape will be attached
>   once you have completed your selection you can begin your editing.

window 2

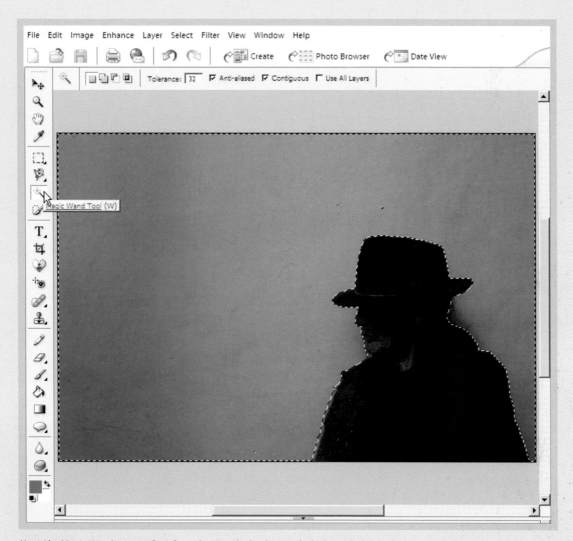

File   Edit   Image   Enhance   Layer   Select   Filter   View   Window   Help

Create   Photo Browser   Date View

Tolerance: 32   ☑ Anti-aliased   ☑ Contiguous   ☐ Use All Layers

Magic Wand Tool (W)

Here the Magic Wand was perfect for selecting the background which needed
toning down

TO SELECT A SHAPE BY THE COLOUR OF THE PIXEL

Often you want to change the colour or adjust the
brightness of a particular area according to areas with
a similar colour. For example, think of a sky and all its
irregular patterns – it would take ages to 'draw' a
selection with your mouse. However, luckily we have a
tool – the **Magic Wand Tool** – which helps us out.

1   Open your image
2   click on the **Magic Wand Tool**
3   click on the area you want to select
>   the **Tolerance** levels in the **Tool Options** bar will allow
    you to adjust the degree of colour that is selected
    within a range of 0 to 255. A low value selects
    colours similar to the pixel you click on; a higher
    value will select a greater range of colours
>   it is best to keep the other options checked
>   **Anti–Aliased** will give your selection a smooth edge
>   **Contiguous** will select pixels of the same colour only
    adjacent to the one you select.

COLOUR BALANCE

As we saw earlier, different light produces different colours. The light of a lamp, for example, will create a much warmer light (more reds) while the light from a cloudy day will be much colder (more blues).

While your digital camera will help – as discussed you can set the **White Balance** to the light around you – often it will misjudge a situation, leaving you having to 'tweak' your image.

This is where Photoshop Elements comes to the rescue. What we want to see is our image illuminated by white light. Remember this will take some time because you need to experiment with what works the best. Be patient: try to concentrate on the skin tone in a portrait and the sky in a landscape. From these starting points you will radically improve the look of your image.

Again there are a number of different ways in which you can adjust the colour balance.

For the easiest way, use the **Auto** modes.

1 Open your image
2 click on **Enhance**
3 click on **Auto Color Correction** (window 1)
4 click on **Save As**.

This may be enough but it doesn't allow you much control. For more control, open your image and:

1 Click on **Enhance**
2 click on **Adjust Color**

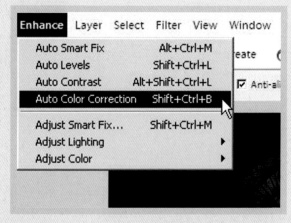

window 1

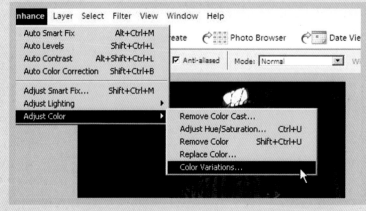

window 2

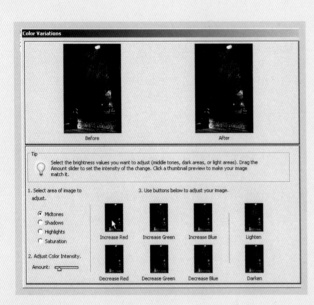

window 3

4   click on **Color Variations** (window 2)
> the box will show you a **Before** and **After** thumbnail,
a choice of the areas of an image you want to adjust
– the **Midtones, Shadows, Highlights** or **Saturation**
and degree of **Intensity** of the colour changes
> finally you have eight boxes allowing you to increase
and decrease the **Red, Green, Blue** and **Lightness** of
the image
> if you want to work on the overall image, click on
Midtones (window 3). I would suggest working at a
low level of intensity to begin with
> now experiment with the colour changes
> by clicking on the **Increase Red** box once the red will
increase. If you click on it again it will increase
slightly more
> once you are happy click on **OK** and you will see your
image edited.

> Remember: If you are unhappy with what you have
done go to Edit and press Undo. You can then start
again. And don't forget that you can work on
selected areas as discussed in the last chapter,
which will show up in the thumbnail box.

MAKING COLOUR CORRECTIONS USING THE QUICK FIX:
1 Open your image
2 click on **Quick Fix**
3 move your mouse down to the **Color** section: clicking
on **Auto** might give you want you want
> if it doesn't, use the sliders on **Temperature** (window
4) to make the image warmer (more red) or colder
(more blue)
> use the sliders on **Tint** to add more green or
magenta to the image.

> Remember: With Quick Edit you can only work on
the whole image and not on a selected area as
you can with the Color Variations option.

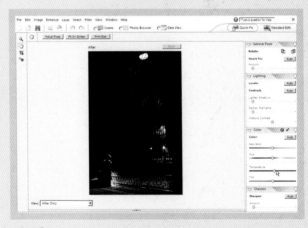

window 4

OVEREXPOSURE AND UNDEREXPOSURE

Because of imperfect light meters, changing light situations, the camera's limitations and our own we often find that our images (or parts of them) are too bright or too dark. Even if an image looks unrecoverable there are a number of tools and options available to us that can improve matters – never give up.

When an image, or part of it, is too bright we call it overexposed: this means that the shadows may not be dark enough and the image may be pale, without the contrast we talked about earlier. When an image is too dark we say it is underexposed: where the highlights are too dark, there is too much contrast and a lack of detail.

As always there are a number of ways you can improve your images. Which one you choose depends on your particular problem, your level of confidence and the amount of time you have available.

In the **Quick Fix** mode you can use either the sliders to lighten the shadows, which will increase the brightness of the dark areas, or you can darken the highlights which will reduce the brightness of the light areas. While this is quick and easy, there is little control over your image.

In the **Standard Edit** mode there are five areas which help us adjust the exposure of our image or parts of our image. The easiest is similar to the above but allows you to work on a selected area.

1   Select the area you need to edit using the **Marquee** or **Magic Wand** tools
2   click on **Enhance**
3   click on **Adjust Lighting**
4   click on **Shadows/Highlights** (window 1)
>   here you can adjust shadows, highlights and mid-tones of your selected area (window 2).

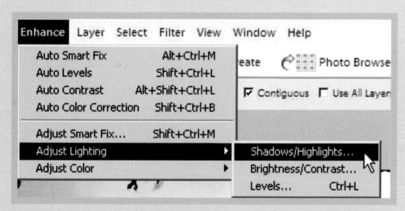

window 1

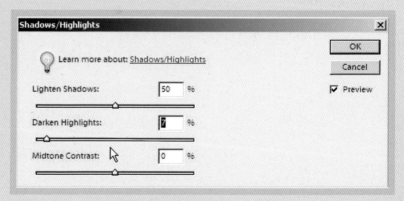

window 2

LEVELS

The **Levels** box shows us a histogram of our image – this graph (window 4) shows us the range of tones our image contains, from the shadows on the left through the midtones in the middle and finally the highlights on the right.

Adjustments using levels improve the tonal range of the image, as well as adding more impact to it. You are in complete control because you use the sliders to alter the shadows, mid-tones and highlights.

A well-exposed image will show a histogram with no gaps and a few gentle peaks. If the peaks are more to the left (i.e. near the shadows) your image is probably underexposed. If the peaks are to the right (i.e. near the highlights) your image is probably overexposed.

Don't worry if you have these one-sided peaks because often you will have a perfectly shot picture. It just happens to be dark or light not too dark or too light. However, if there are gaps showing in your histogram it means there is a lack of information or data, which will make editing more difficult.

Make sure the **Preview** box is ticked and you will see the changes to your image as you edit.

1 Open your image
2 click on **Enhance**
3 click on **Adjust Lighting** (window 3)
4 click on **Levels**
5 click on **Auto-Levels**
> this takes the darkest pixel to its
   darkest black and the brightest pixel
   to its maximum white
6 press **OK** if you are happy.

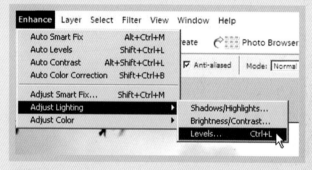

window 3

While this is the easiest option it doesn't, however, allow for your own control.

Instead of clicking on **Auto-Levels**, experiment with using the three sliders (window 4) to achieve the correct exposure and impact.

> try to be as subtle as possible; small
   changes are better than dramatic
   ones
> try to achieve an even histogram but,
   most importantly, watch the image
   itself for the best results.

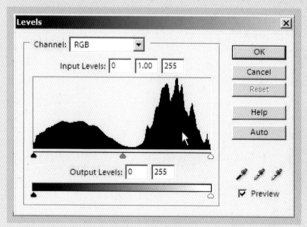

window 4

CURVES

While Photoshop Elements does not have the **Curves** function it is important to take you through this important tool because most other editing software has it.

Like **Levels**, **Curves** affects the brightness of your image. It also adjusts the overall tone of the image and can add contrast and adjust the colour.

The **Curves** box represents the tones of your image by a diagonal line running from the lightest tones (the highlights) to the darkest tones (the shadows) with the mid-tones in between. The horizontal axis shows the current brightness of the pixels whilst the vertical axis shows the amount of change.

1 Open your image
2 click on **Image**
3 click on **Adjustments**
4 click on **Curves**
> **Auto-Curves** may give you what you want but I suggest experimenting by running your mouse pointer along the curve to achieve the best results
> you can make **Colour Changes** by clicking on the **Channel** box and selecting either **Red**, **Blue** or **Green**.

window 1

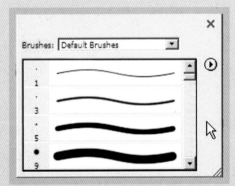

window 2

BURNING AND DODGING TOOL

This tool, found in your **Toolbar** by clicking on its icon or pressing **O**, is great for adding subtle adjustments to selected areas of your image. Even if you have exposed your image perfectly there will still be areas that need some 'help' because digital cameras sometimes struggle to pick up sharp contrast or light differences.

These terms come from the old darkroom days when parts of the image were exposed to more light, 'burning' or less light, 'dodging'. It is the same in our editing software except here you are increasing and decreasing the density of the pixels. Unlike the fiddly efforts in the darkroom, Photoshop Elements allows us much more accuracy. We can make fine adjustments and work on very detailed areas.

Landscapes can often be a problem because a digital camera can struggle to capture the differences between the darkness of the ground and the lightness of the sky.

1 Open your image
2 click on the **Zoom** tool (or select the area you need to edit using the **Marquee** or **Magic Wand** tools)
3 select the area you want to work on remembering that it is best to work on smaller rather than larger areas
4 starting with darkening the sky click the **Burn Tool** (window 1)
5 go to the **Tool Options** bar
6 select one of the **Brushes** (window 2) – a soft-edged brush is often best
7 select the size of the brush
8 select the **Range** – NB: when burning highlights set to mid-tones or shadows; when burning mid-tones or shadows set to highlights; when dodging, always set to highlights
9 select the right **Feather** setting remembering that it is always advisable to work as subtly as possible (I would suggest working at 10 per cent or less as this will give you more control)
10 hold and drag your mouse over the selected area, repeating when necessary.

Repeat as necessary with the **Dodge Tool**.

The third option is the **Sponge Tool** – this increases the **Saturation** in your selected area.

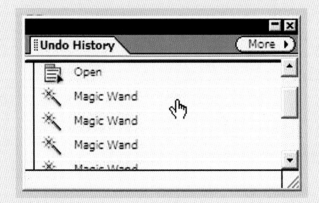

window 3

THE HISTORY WINDOW

When making multiple alterations to an image or part of an image, as you might when using the **Burn** and **Dodge** tools, the **History Window** allows us to backtrack over the changes we have made. While the **Undo** option (under **Edit**) will undo our last action, this window allows us to move between all the changes we have made.

1 Click on **Window**
2 click on **Undo History**
> all your actions to date will be displayed (window 3)
> if you click on a past action it will take you back to how the image looked at that time; this enables you to start again if necessary.

LAYERS

One of the most interesting, but at times tricky, tools to use is **Layers** (see below and window 4). **Layers** allows you to work on one element of an image without affecting the others.

Think of layers as transparent sheets placed over your original image, allowing you to work on individual aspects

of your image without affecting the original or 'background' image – this means if you make a mistake you can easily go back.

Layers can appear complicated but if you use burning and dodging as a start you can see how relatively straightforward they can be.

LAYER PALETTE

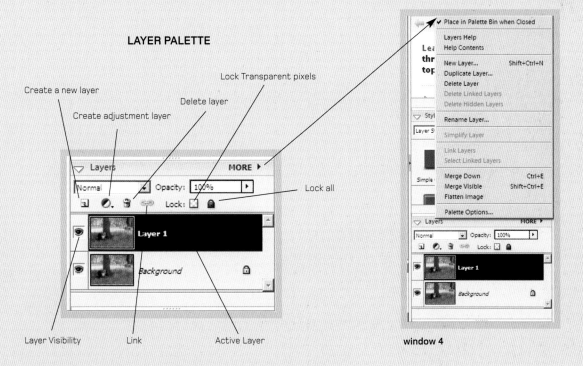

Create a new layer

Create adjustment layer

Delete layer

Lock Transparent pixels

Lock all

Layer Visibility

Link

Active Layer

window 4

BURNING AND DODGING USING LAYERS

While the burning and dodging tools are useful they
often leave results looking flat.

1   Open your image
2   go to **Window** and click on the **Layers** palette
3   get a copy of your image by clicking **Layer** and then
    Duplicate Layer (window 1) or hold and drag the
    background image up to the **New Layer** icon
>   this will create a **Duplicate Layer**
4   click on the **Background** layer (the original layer)
    – a paintbrush will appear next to the **Eye** icon
    (window 2)
5   click on **Enhance**
6   click on **Adjust Lighting**

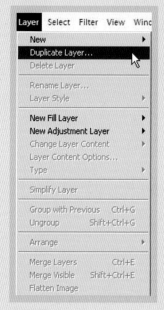

window 1

window 2

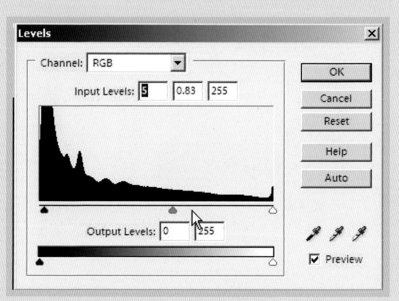

window 3

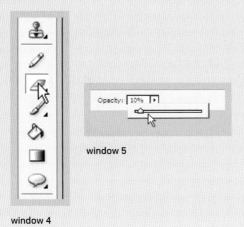

window 5

window 4

7 click on **Levels** (window 3)

8 click on **Overexpose** the image

9 press **OK**

10 click on the top layer called **Background Copy**

11 click on the **Eraser Tool** (window 4)

12 select the **Brush** and **Size** depending on the area

13 set the **Opacity** (window 5) to 10 per cent or under, remembering that the subtle approach is best (the **Opacity** option works in the same way as the **Feather** tool)

14 hold and drag the mouse over the area you want to **Dodge** and you will see the image change

> to save the layers in your image you need to either save your file as a **TIFF** or go to **Layer** then **Flatten Image** as this will allow you to save as a **JPEG**.

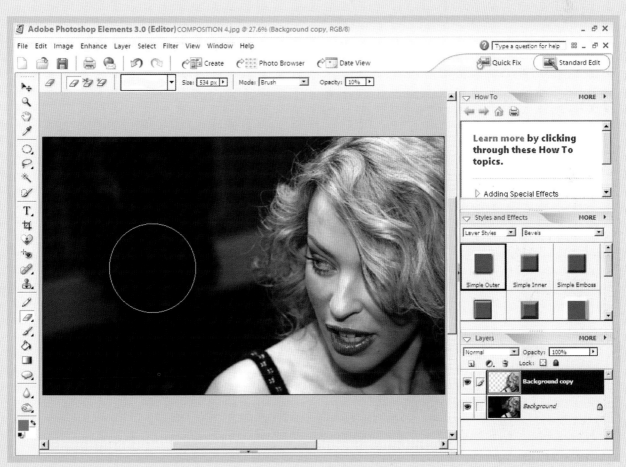

The final image is served better by having a darker background thereby bringing out the face and expression of the pop star, Kylie

UNSHARP MASK

This technique allows us to give the illusion of greater detail by increasing the contrast between the light and dark areas of an image. It is a great tool for adding impact to parts of our image: for example, the eyes in a portrait.

STANDARD EDIT MODE

1   Open your image
2   select the area for sharpening
3   click on **Filters**
4   click on **Sharpen**
5   click on **Unsharp Mask** (window 1)
>   make sure the **Preview** box is ticked
>   use the mouse to select and show the area you need to sharpen. Experiment with the amount – somewhere between 50 and 150 should be sufficient
>   **Radius** governs the number of pixels that will be affected and should be set at between 1 and 2 for high resolution images, higher for lower ones
>   **Threshold** determines the degree to which surrounding pixels are affected: raise the value to limit the effect to edges or if sharpening begins to add any distortion to your image
>   for printing purposes it is advisable to **Over–Sharpen**.

The other **Filters** found in the **Sharpen** option – **Sharpen** (window 2), **Sharpen Edges** and **Sharpen More** – are all **Auto** settings and as such should be used carefully.

This is ideal when you need to sharpen part of an image.

1   Open your image
2   create a **Duplicate Layer** by clicking on **Layer** then **Duplicate Layer** or dragging the background layer to the **New Layer** icon
3   click on the **Background Layer** (the original and bottom layer)
4   click on **Filter**
5   click on **Sharpen**
6   click on **Unsharp Mask**: increase the amount to around 200 (window 3)
7   click on **Background Copy**
8   click on the **Eraser Tool**
9   select the **Brush** and its **Size**
>   use a subtle **Opacity** of 10 per cent and hold and drag over the area you want to sharpen
>   increase the Opacity if you need to.

You can see the difference you are making by clicking off the **Eye** in the **Background** layer:
1   Click on **Layer**
2   click on **Flatten Image**
3   save as required.

TO USE UNSHARP MASK WITH LAYERS

window 1

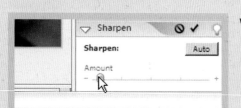

window 2

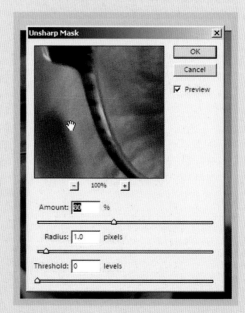

window 3

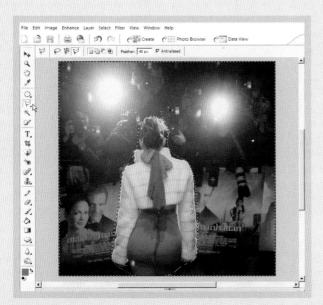

window 4

GAUSSIAN BLUR

Another way to make part of the image stand out is to blur the background – this reduces the distracting detail and moves the eye to the main subject.

1 Open your image
2 select the background area using the **Marquee** tools or the **Magic Wand** (window 4)
3 **Feather** the selected area to blur the changes or difference you are making (window 5)
4 click on **Filter**
5 click on **Blur**
6 click on **Gaussian Blur** (window 6)
> enter the amount or use the slider according to your needs (window 7)
7 save as required.

window 7

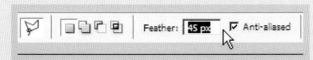

window 5

window 6

GAUSSIAN BLUR USING LAYERS

1 Open your image
2 create a **Duplicate Layer** (see page 76)
3 click on **Background** layer
4 click on **Filter**
5 click on **Blur**
6 click on **Gaussian Blur**; enter the amount
7 click on **Background Copy** layer
8 click on the **Eraser** tool
9 select a suitable **Brush** and **Size**
> use the required amount of **Opacity**
10 erase up to the edges of your foreground subject
11 save as required.

Experiment with the other filter options such as **Artistic** and **Sketch**.

TEXT TOOL

The **Text Tool** allows us to write on our images – this makes it so easy to create your own birthday cards, get well cards and image messages to email and send around the world.

1 Open your image
2 click on the **Text Tool**
3 select the way you want the text to go – horizontally or vertically – by using your mouse or pressing **T** to scroll through the options (window 1)
4 select the other options such as the **Font** (window 2), the **Size** of the type and the **Color**
5 click on the image where you want to begin – this will automatically create another layer

6 type the required text (window 3)
> if you want to write in more than one place click **Once** to end the first edit and click **Again** to open a new layer and the chance to write more.

There are many types of effects you can add by clicking on the **Warp Text** and seeing what you can come up with.

window 1

window 2

window 3

COLOUR TO BLACK AND WHITE

Some cameras have a black and white setting – I would personally avoid this because because there is less data, which impacts on your manipulation options when it comes to editing. It is easier and better to 'think' in black and white and convert to black and white in Photoshop Elements.

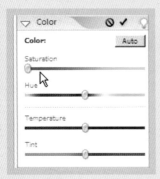

window 4

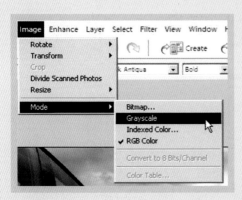

window 5

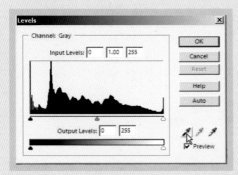

window 6

QUICK FIX – the easiest way

1   Open your image
2   click on the **Quick Fix** mode
3   go to the **Lighting** box and, with your mouse, drag the **Saturation** slider all the way to the left (window 4). This causes the image to lose all its colour information
4   add more contrast to the image by adjusting the **Lighten Shadows** and **Darken Highlights** sliders
5   **Save As**.

An easy way in the STANDARD EDIT mode

1   Open your image
2   click on the **Standard Edit** mode
3   go to **Image**
4   scroll down to **Mode**
5   click on **Grayscale** (window 5)
6   go to **Enhance**
7   scroll to **Adjust Lighting**
8   go to **Brightness/Contrast** and adjust according to requirements
>   go again to **Enhance** and **Adjust Lighting** if you feel you need to
8   go to **Levels**
9   adjust the **Tone** of the image.

A further addition to the LEVELS choice

1   Go to **Levels**
2   click on the first **Eyedropper** icon (in the box, just below **Auto**) entitled **Set Black Point** (window 6)
3   move your mouse pointer around the image and click on a spot that is black. This will set the black tone for the rest of the image
4   do the same with the far right **Eyedropper** entitled **Set White Point**
5   **Save As**.

> Remember: Contrast is vital for a black and white image, otherwise there is a tendency for the image to appear flat.

COLOUR TO BLACK AND WHITE USING LAYERS

1 Open your image
2 go to **Layer**
3 scroll down to **New Adjustment Layer**
4 go across to **Hue/Saturation** (window 1)
5 when the **Hue/Saturation** box appears,
   simply click **OK**
6 create another **Hue/Saturation Layer**
7 go to **Layer**
8 then to **Duplicate Layer**.

You should now have three layers in total; the original
Background Layer and two **Hue/Saturation
Adjustment** layers.

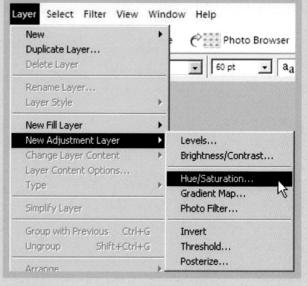

window 1

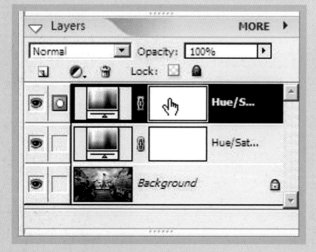

window 2

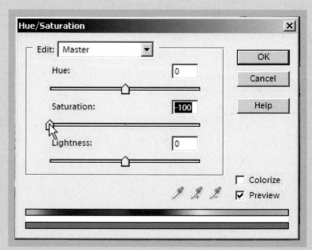

window 3

9 Now click on the top layer – the second one you created (window 2)
10 double-click on the **Layer** thumbnail icon; the **Hue/Saturation** box should appear
11 drag the **Saturation** slider down to minus 100 (window 3)
12 click on the bottom new layer (i.e. the first adjustment layer you created)
13 click on the **Mode** box in the top left hand corner of the layer box and scroll down and select **Color** (window 4)
14 double-click on the **Layer** thumbnail icon
15 adjust the **Hue** slider according to what you want (window 5)
16 create a new **Adjustment Layer** (as above) but instead of **Hue/Saturation** choose the **Levels** adjustment layer (window 6)
17 use the sliders to make fine adjustments to your image
18 save as required.

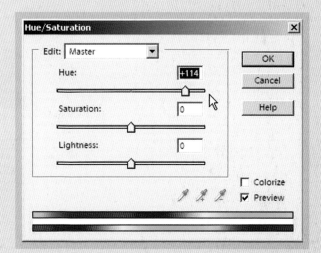

window 5

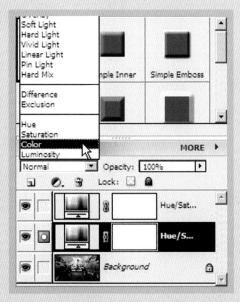

window 4

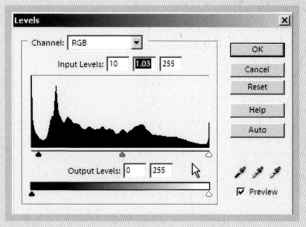

window 6

DUOTONES

As well as changing your colour images to black
and white you can also easily change them into
'duotone' images.

window 1

1 Open your image
2 click on **Enhance**
3 scroll down to **Adjust Color**, and move your mouse
   across to **Remove Color Cast**
4 go back to **Enhance**
5 scroll down to **Adjust Color**
6 move your mouse over to the right and select **Color
   Variations** (window 1)
7 click on the **Midtones**
8 use the **Increase** and **Decrease** buttons to change
   the colour according to your taste (window 2)

window 2

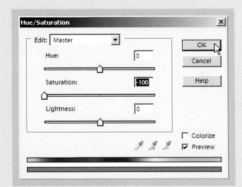

window 3

window 4

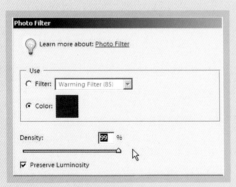

window 5

CREATING DUOTONES USING LAYERS

1 Open your image
2 click on **Enhance**
3 scroll down to **Adjust Color**
4 move on to **Adjust Hue/Saturation**
5 drag the **Saturation** slider all the way down
   (window 3)
6 click **OK**
7 go to **Layers**
8 click on **New Adjustment Layer**
9 go to **Photo Filters**
10 click **OK**
> the box shown should have both the **Filters** and the
   Preview box should be ticked
11 scroll through the **Filter** options to decide which
   colour you want to choose (window 4)
12 use the **Density** slider to adjust the strength of the
   filter(window 5)
13 click on **OK**
14 save as required.

CLONING AND SPOT HEALING

More often than you would like you find dust and marks on your digital images that you would sooner be without. Luckily it is very easy to remove these unwanted blemishes without too much hassle.

USING THE SPOT HEALING BRUSH

1 Open your image
2 **Zoom** in on the area with the blemish
3 select the **Spot Healing Brush** (window 1)
4 select an adequate sized **Brush** to cover the blemish
5 select a **Type** option depending on which works best: **Proximity Match** uses the pixels around the edge of a selected area, while the **Create Texture** uses the all the pixels in the surrounding area
6 hold the mouse click down, drag the mouse pointer over the blemish and watch it disappear.

USING THE CLONE STAMP TOOL

The clone tool duplicates pixels so you can copy one area and paste it over another: great for dust, unwanted telegraph poles or distracting objects in the background. It also gives you much more control than the **Spot Healing Brush**.

1 Open your image
2 **Zoom** in on the area you want to clone
3 select the **Clone Stamp** tool
4 in the tool options bar select the type of **Brush**
5 select the **Size** of the brush
6 select the **Mode** option; this determines how the pattern blends with existing pixels; I would suggest using the **Replace** mode as it preserves film grain and stops the cloned area looking too flat
7 click on **Aligned** to make sure the area moves as you move the mouse
8 click on a neighbouring area and then hold and drag over the area you wish to remove
9 save as required.

window 1

window 2

window 3

RED-EYE REDUCTION

The effect of red-eye on portraits of people (and sometimes white- and green-eye when photographing animals) is caused by the reflection of the camera flash from the retina.

It is an irritating problem and in the past the ruin of many portraits – however, again Photoshop Elements comes to the rescue and makes it very easy for us to remove this problem.

1   Open your image
2   **Zoom** into the area around the eyes
3   select the **Red-Eye Reduction** tool with your mouse (window 4)
4   draw a selection around the eye by holding and dragging your mouse
>   when you release the mouse the red-eye should be removed (window 5)
5   save as required.

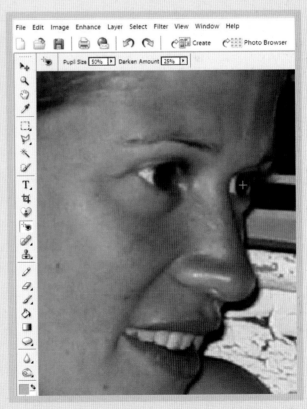

window 4

window 5

PRINTING YOUR IMAGES

While the digital world allows us to share our pictures online you could be forgiven for thinking there is no need to bother with old-fashioned prints. But after all your hard work in editing the pictures, there is nothing better than having a tangible photograph in your hands.

You now need to know how to print out your works of art successfully and show them off to friends and family.

6.0 PRINTING YOUR IMAGES

PRINTING EQUIPMENT AND FACILITIES

PRINTERS

Modern ink-jet printers offer marvellous results for relatively cheap prices but it is the paper which is the real dictator of quality. Ink-jet printers work by using microscopic droplets of ink fired from hundreds of tiny nozzles inside the printer. The ink is stored in separate compartments which can be refilled when necessary.

Factors to consider when choosing your printer:

* what is the maximum size paper you will want or need to print?
* how many different coloured inks are used? More than six will give you the best results though fewer can still be effective
* how high a resolution will you need (though you may find it difficult to see the difference between 1440 and 2800 dpi)?

PRINTING PAPER

Like the relationship between the camera and the lens – where the lens dictates the quality – the most important thing to consider when printing is the paper you use. You can buy a wide range of paper and it's best to experiment with ones you like and which work for you. Gloss (shiny) and matt (non-shiny) are the two main areas of paper choice.

PRINTING AWAY FROM HOME

If you don't have a printer or find the time and expense of fiddling with inks and settings too much like hard work there are other options available to you:

The high street: a number of different high-street processing stores will take images (both edited and un-edited) from your camera, memory card or CD and print acceptable images.

Online Printing: a growing number of online sites will print your images without you having to leave the comfort of your own home. Just simply register and follow the instructions.

Now to look at printing from home...

COLOUR

COLOUR CONSISTENCY

The colour gamut is the phrase you use to describe the range of colours a device has, be it a scanner, a printer or a monitor, and unfortunately they are not consistent. Two different monitors will display a different version of the same image. But this difference is especially marked when you compare monitors and printers. This is because they use different means to display their images. A monitor uses light whereas a printer uses dyes and ink to display the image.

You can keep adjusting the image until you get the result you need, however, this 'trial and error' approach is a waste of paper and time and of course only applies to that one image. What happens when you want to print off the next image? You need, therefore, to find a way of getting consistent colors between your monitor and your printer.

COLOUR MANAGEMENT

You can achieve this simply in Photoshop Elements with **Color Settings**.
Before you edit any image go to Photoshop Elements:
1   Click on **Color Settings**
2   click on **Full Color Management**
3   click on **Edit Your Image**
4   click on **Prepare For Printing**.

PRINTING

CHECKLIST BEFORE PRINTING

- Make sure you have chosen the correct paper for your needs
- correct the image for printing remembering to make images slightly brighter because printers are generally not great at producing darker tones
- increase the saturation of your image because printing often makes the image look duller than it did on screen
- make sure you have the correct image size and resolution for your needs.

PRINTING YOUR IMAGES

Once you have your image edited and ready to go:

1 Click on **File**, then **Print**
> the **Print Preview** box will appear
2 select the **Size** of the image to be printed
> in the **Print Size** options you have a choice of the actual size based on the document itself; certain preset sizes set to fit on the page – depending on the size of paper you choose – and a custom size where you make your own settings
> if you use the custom setting make sure the **Show Bounding Box** is ticked because this will allow you to scale the image manually using the handles on the edges of the preview thumbnail

> the **Centre Image** box should usually be ticked to make sure the image stays in the centre of the page but if you **Untick** it you can move the image around freely as required
> the **Border** box will allow you to select the size and colour of a border.

You also have the chance to include a **File Name** and **Caption** on your printed page.

1 Make sure the **Show More Options** box is ticked
2 select the **Show More Options** box and choose **Color Management**
3 select **Document** as **Source Space**
4 select your printer profile as the **Print Space**
5 click on the **Page Setup** button
> boxes differ between Windows and Macs, but you should be able to set **Paper Size** and **Position** (horizontal or vertical)
> the correct printer will be selected automatically
6 click on **OK**
7 return to **Print Dialog** box
8 click on **Print**
9 click on **Properties**
10 turn **Printer Color Management** off
11 click on **OK**
12 click on **Print**.

And that's about it. This is, after all, only a basic guide to digital photography but I hope by now, or at least once you've read this book and familiarized yourself with it, you will begin to love the art of taking, editing and printing your own digital photographs. Have fun!

TROUBLESHOOTING

CAMERA STOPS OPERATING
- some cameras will turn themselves off automatically – give it a few moments to start up
- check that the batteries are installed correctly and fully charged – this can be a problem particularly when using the camera in a cold environment
- clean the electrical contacts with a lint-free cloth
- make sure the memory card door is closed correctly
- if the internal system is not working properly, the camera may have to be replaced.

MEMORY CARD WILL NOT FORMAT
- gently blow on the contacts of the memory card to remove dust
- insert the card a few times because the sliding action is designed to polish the contacts
- the camera's 'protection' mode is switched on.

CAMERA WILL NOT SHOOT ANY MORE IMAGES
- make sure you have inserted a memory card correctly
- you have run out of space on your memory card
- try setting a lower resolution if you do not want to erase any images
- make sure the camera is set to the 'shoot still images' mode and not the 'movie' mode found on some digital cameras.

CAMERA WILL NOT DISPLAY THE IMAGES
- make sure the LCD screen is turned on
- make sure the correct 'display' mode has been turned on to allow you to review your images
- make sure you haven't removed the memory card while the camera was still downloading. If you have you may have damaged the card
- if you have uploaded edited images from your computer – the camera is unable to display edited images.

YOU CANNOT DELETE AN IMAGE
- the image is protected. You can unlock this protection from the display menu.

CAMERA WILL NOT DOWNLOAD OR WORKS ERRATICALLY
- make sure you have installed the camera's software on your computer
- the USB driver is not installed
- make sure your USB or Firewire lead is connected properly to your computer
- your connection leads might be faulty
- if you are downloading using your camera make sure the battery level is not too low to operate.

A-Z GLOSSARY

Analogue: image proportionate to some other physical property or change

Aperture: controls the amount of light coming through the lens and affects the depth of field: what's in and out of focus

Back-up: save to second source (e.g. CDs)

Bit: a binary digit: 1 or 0 – basic unit of computer information

Bleed: when a photograph, line or colour runs off the page

Brightness Range: between light and dark

Brush: types and size of brushes from various different palettes, use to clone, dodge, burn, etc.

Buffer: time it takes to download an image to camera, printer, computer

Burning: gives area more exposure, makes it darker

Byte: unit of digital information. 1 byte equals 8 bits

Cache: RAM dedicated to each part of a computer

Calibration: when you attempt to match features – e.g. the colours, of a monitor and a printer

Camera Exposure: amount of light reaching the light sensors

Capacity: quantity of data able to be stored on computer, CD or memory card measured in MB or GB

Cartridge: casing to protect ink or film

CD-ROM: Compact Disk-Read Only Memory Storage device for images, etc.

Cloning: copying pixels from one area of an image to another

CMYK: Cyan Magenta Yellow Black. Primaries used to create a sense of colour

Cold colours: blues and cyans

Colourize: add colour to a greyscale image, no loss of lightness

Colour Sync: colour management software which matches colours from monitor to printer

Colour Gamut: range of colours a printer, camera or monitor can reproduce

Colour Management: matching colours between systems – e.g. monitor and printer

Compact Flash: one of many different types of memory card

Complementary Colours: Pair of colours which produce white – i.e. the primary colours (red, green, blue) match the secondary colours (cyan, magenta, yellow)

Compression: reducing the size of a file

Contrast: the difference between the light tones (highlights) and dark tones (shadows) of an image

Crop: re-sizing or re-shaping of an image

CPU: Central Processing Unit – processes the information captured on the image sensor

Cyan: blue-green – complementary colour is red

Data: information used by a camera or computer

Default: the standard settings on your camera and computer

Depth of Field: the area that is still 'sharp' in front of and behind the focused point. Affected by the aperture, the focal length and image magnification

Digital Zoom: where the camera 'crops' the image, reducing its size but magnifying what you see

Dodging: gives the image less exposure, making it lighter

Dpi: dots per inch: measure of resolution of a printer or monitor

A-Z GLOSSARY

Duotone: reproducing an image with two colours

Exposure: the amount of light falling on the camera sensor measured by the combination of the shutter speed and aperture

f Number: settings which determine the aperture. f2.8 is a wide aperture which lets in lots of light, f22 a narrow aperture which lets in less light

Feathering: blurs editing changes or suddenness of the changes

Files: different files are used for different purposes. For example, a JPEG is used for images whilst a .DOC is used for words

Filter: alters the appearance of an image – can either be attached to the camera or 'faked' using your editing software

Firewire: provides rapid communication between devices

Focal Length: lens magnification: i.e. what you can see

Focus: adjusting the lens to keep the subject sharp

Format: to permanently delete the contents of your memory card

Greyscale: a black and white image

Histogram: a graph showing the complete tonal range of an image from shadows through to mid-tones to highlights

Hue: what you see as a colour

Interpolation: used to give the appearance of an increase in resolution or size by increasing the number of pixels

Kelvin: the measure of colour temperature

Lasso: the tool used to draw a freehand selection around part of an image

LCD: liquid crystal display

Mac: common abbreviation for an Apple Macintosh computer

Marquee: the outline of dots to show a selected area

Mask: select part of an image for editing

Megapixel: the measure of a camera's resolution

Memory Card: an electronic chip inside a plastic casing

Metering: measuring what exposure is needed

Noise: unwanted electronic interference which affects the image; occurs most often in low light conditions

Opacity: the degree or the strength of various tools

Pixel: PICture ELement: the smallest unit of digital imaging

Ppi: pixels per inch a measure of the resolution of images and printers

Primary Colours: red, blue and green

RAM: random access memory. The storage of data on your computer

Re-sizing: altering the size or resolution of an image

RGB: red, green and blue

Resolution: a measure of the amount of information or data in an image or printer

Saturation: the degree of grey in a colour. Dictates the 'strength' of a colour

Shutter Lag: the delay between pressing the shutter button and the image being captured digitally

Shutter Speed: the length of time the sensor is exposed to light

Thumbnail: a small, low-resolution version of a larger file

USB: Universal Serial Bus. One of a few types of connections between a camera, a card reader, a scanner, a printer and a computer

Viewfinder: the hole through which you compose your image

White Balance: an adjustment on the camera to make sure colours are captured correctly depending on their source

INDEX

A
action mode 21, 30
action shots 44-5
aperture 27
aperture priority 21, 30
auto adjustment mode 21
auto-exposure mode 20, 30

B
beach mode 21
black and white 43, 81-3
box brownie 8
bridge camera 20
brush tools 54
burning and dodging 74, 76-7

C
candle mode 21
Capa, Robert 34
cityscapes 42
cloning 86
colour balance 70-1
colour consistency 90
colour management 90
colour to black and white 81-3
colour versus black and white 43
compact camera 20
compact flash 23
composition 34
computers
   choice 48
   copying and saving 49
   downloading from camera 48
   downloading from card reader 49
   downloading to computer 48-9
   duplicate images 49
   filing system importance 49
control dial 21
cookie cutter tool 61
crop tool 61
cropping 57
curves 74

D
depth of field 28
digital cameras
   bridge camera 20
   choice 18
   compact camera 20
   controls 20-1
   deleting not allowed 92

differences from film-based 14
megapixels 15, 18
not operating 92
parts 12-13
pixels 15
prosumer camera 20
purpose 18
quality measure 15
single lens reflex (SLR) camera 20
symbols for controls 21
viewed from outside 12-13
will not accept more images 92
will not display images 92
will not download 92
working system 14-15
digital photography, advantages and
disadvantages 14
digital zoom 19
display images 21
Doisneau, Robert 34
duotones 84-5

E
editing
   adding impact 64-5
   brush tools 54
   burning and dodging 74, 76-7
   colour balance 70-1
   cropping 57
   curves 74
   feathering 68
   file saving 58-60
   file types 53
   Gaussian blur 79
   history 75
   hue 66-7
   image correction 54, 57
   image selection 54, 55-6
   image selection, part 67
   image stitching 62
   layers tool 75-7
   levels 73
   monitor calibration 52
   panoramas 62-3
   perspective 63
   saturation 66-7
   shape by colour 69
   shape changing 61
   shape, irregular 69
   size changing 59-60
   software choices 53

straightening 57
   text 80
   toolbar 54
   unsharp mask 78
evaluative metering 21
exposure 28-9, 33, 72-3
exposure modes 20

F
f stop 27
feathering 68
file saving 58-60
film-based photography
   differences from digital 14
   disadvantages 8
   outline of system 14
Firewire 48-9
flash 22, 23, 41
flash blur 45
focal length 19
focussing 31

G
Gaussian blur 79
glossary 93-4
golden mean 35
H
hue 66-7

I
invisible lines 36
ISO setting 21, 28-9

L
landscape mode 21, 30
landscapes 42
Lartigue, Jacques-Henri 8
lasso tool 68
layers tool 75-7
LCD screen 20-1
lenses 19, 22
levels 73
lighting 40-1
lines 36

M
macro 30
magic wand tool 69
manual adjustment 21
manual adjustment settings 20
manual operation 18, 30

megapixels 15, 18
memory card
  downloading 23
  options 23
  not formatting 92
  'reusable' 15, 23
memory stick 23
metering 21
microdrive 23
mode dial 21, 30
monitor calibration 52

N
night mode 21
night portrait mode 21

O
optical zoom lens 19
overexposure 33, 72-3

P
panoramas 62-3
panoramic setting 42
perspective 32, 63
Photoshop Elements 52-3, 54
picture taking
  action shots 44-5
  anticipation 34
  basic principles 26-9
  cityscapes 42
  copying other photographers 34
  exposure 33
  focussing 31
  general advice 31
  landscapes 42

lighting 40-1
perspective 32
portraits 37-9
'rule' breaking 34-5
shutter speeds 26, 31
sports shots 44-5
pixels 15
playback mode 21
portrait mode 21, 30
portraits 37-9
ports 22
power on/off control 20
printing
  away from home 90
  checklist and action 91
  colour consistency 90
  colour management 90
  paper 90
  printers 90
processor 20
program 21, 30
prosumer camera 20

R
record mode 21
red-eye reduction 87

S
saturation 66-7
secure digital 23
set-up options 21
shape changing 61
shapes 35
short film capacity 21
shutter button 20

shutter priority 21, 30
shutter speeds 26, 26, 31
'shutter-lag' 20
silhouettes 44
single lens reflex (SLR) camera 20
size changing 59-60
smart media 23
software choices 53
sports shots 44-5
spot healing 86
spot metering 21
straightening 57
symmetry 36-7

T
time-delay 20
troubleshooting 92

U
underexposure 33, 72-3
unsharp mask 78
USB 48-9

V
viewfinder 20

W
white balance 21, 70

X
Xd picture card 23

Z
zoom lenses 19